The Real Meaning
of *Doctor Who*

The Real Meaning of Popular Culture™ series

General Editor: Nicolas Michaud

The Real Meaning of Popular Culture™ series

The Real Meaning of *Doctor Who*

COURTLAND LEWIS

OPEN UNIVERSE
Chicago

To find out more about Open Universe and Carus Books, visit our website at www.carusbooks.com.

Copyright © 2021 by Carus Books

All rights reserved. No part of this publication may be reproduced, stored in a retrieval system, or transmitted, in any form or by any means, electronic, mechanical, photocopying, recording, or otherwise, without the prior written permission of the publisher, Carus Books, 315 Fifth Street, Peru, Illinois 61354.

Printed and bound in the United States of America. Printed on acid-free paper.

The Real Meaning of Doctor Who

ISBN: 978-1-63770-000-6

This book is also available as an e-book (978-1-63770-001-3).

Library of Congress Control Number: 2021941773

Contents

Preface

In order to create a more inclusive book, and to avoid making false statements relating to the Doctor's gender, I will use the following widely accepted pronouns when referring to the Doctor as a totality of all incarnations: 'zie' for 'he/her'; 'zir' for 'him/her'; 'zirs' for 'his/her'; and 'zirself' for 'himself/herself'. As a fictional alien, the Doctor's concept of gender is much different than ours, so it's not clear what exactly is the appropriate pronoun. Regardless, since the Doctor has been played by both men and women, it would be incorrect to refer to the Doctor solely as a man or a woman, and as a writer, it's too clunky to replace every pronoun with 'the Doctor' or 's/he', 'him/her', and so forth. So, to make things easier, and more importantly, correct, I will use the gender-neutral pronouns.

Thanks to writers like Steven Moffat, numbering the Doctors can be difficult. Technically, the War Doctor is the Ninth Doctor, which means Nine, Ten, Eleven, and Twelve are Ten, Eleven, Twelve, and Thirteen; but if you include the half-human Doctor, which Moffat does, then Tennant is Eleven, half-human Tennant is

Twelve, Smith is Thirteen, Capaldi Fourteen, and Whittaker Fifteen. Such numerology might be fun when doing calculus, but it's a little annoying when reading a fun book on *Doctor Who*. As a result, I'll stick with the numbering convention that calls John Hurt's Doctor the "War Doctor," I will exclude the half-human Doctor from the numbering, and start with Christopher Eccleston's Doctor as the Ninth Doctor, ending with Jodie Whittaker as the Thirteenth Doctor.

Finally, I take a fairly loose approach to canon. I'm a fan of all things *Doctor Who*, and instead of getting bogged down in what deserves to be included or excluded from canon, I will simply make reference to whatever I feel is relevant—be that TV, comics, books, audios, or something else. I will leave it to readers to decide whether they accept or reject what I include.

My hope is that each chapter will engage readers young and old, whether you're on your first body or your thirteenth regeneration. What's fun about *Doctor Who* is that its lessons are accessible to everyone, so whether you're a lifelong fan or you have just discovered the series, you should have fun.

For me, *Doctor Who* does more than just entertain. It enlightens and motivates, and I hope that this book will do the same. I'm ready to get started. I hope you are too.

So, let the journey begin—Allons-y!

Welcome Aboard the TARDIS—It's Bigger on the Inside

The purpose of this new series, The Real Meaning of Popular Culture, is to explain how pop culture icons like *Doctor Who* infuse our lives with meaning and provide frameworks for interpreting and understanding our existence in the world. *Doctor Who* not only shapes, but in some ways, creates our reality.

As I began writing this book, I already fully agreed with the purpose of The Real Meaning of Popular Culture, but something happened between the time I began and when I finished writing the book. I became a father! Now, my belief in the purpose of the series is incorrigible. I have seen first-hand how *Doctor Who* infects, shapes, and creates meaning in the world my son inhabits. Sure, he doesn't understand the intricacies of time travel, but at two years old, he grasps the concept of the Doctor being multiple persons, the TARDIS, and the struggle against villains—he's especially worried about the Daleks and Zygons. As he gets older, these lessons will shape how he interprets situations and create the unique worldview that comprises his reality.

It's my hope that, as it was for me, *Doctor Who* will inspire a curiosity about the world, dedication to do what's right in the face of injustice, the acceptance of all other living beings, and a general love of adventure, learning, and maturing as a person. Since you've decided to read this book, I assume *Doctor Who* has probably had a similar impact on your life. My task is to help you explore the specifics of how *Doctor Who* shapes and creates an interpretive framework for understanding all aspects of life. However, if you're new to the Whoniverse, I will help you makes sense of the power of *Doctor Who* in constructing and sustaining a particular view of reality. Either way, you will enjoy the journey of self-discovery that follows. To this end, let's consider the following thought experiment.

Imagine yourself transplanted to a universe where what you take to be reality is completely different from the one you currently enjoy. In this imagined world, maybe objects you see as red they call "blue," maybe the inhabitants of this world only see in two dimensions, and for them they perceive the world upside down, or maybe time moves in reverse. Think about how difficult it would be to interact with the inhabitants of this world, and consider how strange you would be to them. People would struggle to understand you, you would appear to be speaking backwards, and who knows what other awkward situations you would find yourself. Could you learn to survive in this world, or would you be hopelessly lost—an outsider, stranger, oddity, object of ridicule?

If you find yourself freaking out about such a possibility, I'm here to comfort you. You've already experienced such an event, at least once in your life, if not multiple times. At birth, you're "thrown" into a new world, and for several years your body struggles to make sense of all the new sensory information. From language to perception, and everywhere in between, your body continuously works to successfully process its new environment, and if you're lucky, by the time you're three years old, you're pretty good at navigating this new reality.

This process of assimilation occurs on some level anytime we enter a new environment that is completely different from the environment we're used to perceiving, but as we mature, it most often occurs on a psychological level. As we live our lives, we create a running narrative within our minds that explains who we are and what we find meaningful and valuable. In other words, as we live, we organize a set of important memories and beliefs that becomes our mental autobiography. Through the random and planned events of your physical experiences and mental engagement with the environment in which you exist, you create a reality for yourself. This doesn't mean there is no external reality independent of your experiences, but for the most part, our reality is simply the combination of our physical and mental worlds engaged in a particular environment of external stimuli. We create an interpretive framework that we use to make sense of new events, constantly working to create a consistent narrative that becomes our reality. Then, at key points in our lives, when our narrative is challenged by significant events, we're forced to create a new reality. For instance, once you figure things out as a child, your body changes, and now you have to relearn everything as a teenager, then as an adult, and so on.

What does this have to do with *Doctor Who*? Well, when we combine the fact that our physical and psychological experiences of the world create our reality, then we begin to see how significant popular culture is in shaping this reality. As Noël Carroll explains in *Minerva's Night Out*, popular culture is an educator, one that teaches norms and values about wrong and right, normal and abnormal, memes and tropes about meaning, and a paradigm that comprises our framework for interpreting and understanding reality. Not only is popular culture an educator, but as Marcel Danesi notes in *Popular Culture*, pop culture validates everyday experience, creating a sense of community, which further creates communal structures of meaning. When combined, popular culture has the power to create a collective memory and paradigm of meaning that influences every aspect of our lives. So, it's not far-fetched to say that shows like *Doctor Who* have the power to create our reality.

In fact, if you've ever attended a *Doctor Who* convention, then you know first-hand how the show shapes reality. Such gatherings bring together people from all over the world who all have a shared outlook on life. They dress in costumes (cosplay), perform, and spend hours talking about episodes, actors, and anything else you can image. The few special hours spent at these conventions often feel more real that the "real world," because you're immersed in all things *Doctor Who*, which is the imagined world that shaped your reality. We get a taste of this reality when we watch an episode, but conventions (and similar events) validate our beliefs and allow us to experience the realness of *Doctor Who*.

Let me share a story of my own experience of *Doctor Who* shaping reality. When I was very young, two events and one person determined the trajectory of my life. The first event, which is actually my very first memory, was when I drank kerosene—yes, I just said "I drank *kerosene!*" As I vividly recall, I was outside of my grandparents' home and extremely thirsty. As luck would have it, I found an old coffee can of clear liquid. I could tell it was clear because I could see my reflection in the bottom. Because water is clear, I assumed the liquid was water. After taking several gulps, my world went blank. I was comatose for several days, kept alive in an oxygen tent. This near-death experience was a traumatic event that made me appreciate the fragility and value of life. It planted in me a seed that grew into a full-blown wonderment of life, enjoyment of laughing, an appreciation of vulnerability, and the desire to ponder, know, and experience all that exists—no matter how scary or strange.

Closely related to the wonder produced by drinking kerosene is the person and second event that greatly influenced my life—my grandfather and *Doctor Who.* Both comprise the memory of my childhood. Growing up, I spent a lot of time with my grandfather. He drove me around town visiting different hardware stores, took me on jobs (like preaching, plumbing, farming, pest control, electrical work, and locksmithing), we experimented on food, which usually involved adding different liquids to ice cream or putting Miracle Whip on something (black-eyed peas, toast, corn bread, etc.), played an assortment of word games, he told lots of jokes, often from *Reader's Digest*, and of course, we watched TV. It was he who introduced me to *Doctor*

Who when I was six years old, and it was typically at his house that I watched each Saturday night on our local PBS station in 1983.

Kerosene spurred an appreciation and enjoyment of life, *Doctor Who* structured and focused the resulting passion, and my grandfather gave me a real-life example of how one should live. Watching *Doctor Who*, while lying on the floor of my grandparents' house, was sacred, like going to church—except much more interesting! Each week I found myself immersed and mystified by the strange new realities of *Doctor Who*. The episodes I remember are sacred relics of my childhood, and they still influence me forty years later. They taught me how to interpret the world, which means *Doctor Who* is the framework for how I construct my reality. It taught me that existence is as infinite as I want it to be, both in terms of the external world but also in terms of my internal imagination and life's potential. It challenged my understanding of right and wrong, it changed the way I understood the nature of the universe, how I treated people, and it gave me hope in a future where I (and everyone else) might flourish.

The purpose of this book is to show that *Doctor Who* creates a framework in which to interpret all aspects of life. As the famous sociologist Max Weber explained in the early 1900s, family, friends, and traditions influence much of our beliefs. Fast-forward one hundred years, and popular culture tends to hold greater influence than any other force. Factor in nearly sixty years of serials, episodes, books, comics, and a whole host of other goodies, and we should not be surprised by *Doctor Who*'s impact on individuals and the culture.

Yet, it's still amazing how a television show about a time traveling alien can have such a tremendous impact on the lives of so many. From people who saw the first episode, to my two-year-old son, *Doctor Who* has not only shaped the world by introducing names and creating pop culture themes, but it has shaped the minds of countless millions of adults and children. Along with Elvis Presley and the Beatles, *Doctor Who* is arguably the most influential pop culture icon since mass media began in the early 1900s, and it is time we examine how deep its influence runs.

The Examined and the Good Life

The good life is a concept that doesn't get much attention these days, but early philosophers like Socrates and Aristotle thought that determining the good life was one of the most important tasks for humans. What is the good life? The good life is not just some random way of living that makes you feel good. Rather, it's a prescription for how to live the best possible life, one of happiness and flourishing. From Socrates and Confucius, to Jesus and Mohammad, great thinkers have pondered how humans should live. I don't mean these great thinkers sat around coming up with rules that everyone should follow, nor do I mean something similar to the self-help, prosperity gospel of the recent decades that teaches how, "You too, can have pleasure and money, if you follow these simple rules and buy my book!" These, and countless other thinkers, sought to discover the truth about how we should live our lives, whether we're rich or poor, abled or disabled, popular or merely a loner. The good life attempts to understand the meaning of life and how it is applied to each person's subjective experience with the world.

The good life in no way guarantees pleasure and ease, but it gives you a framework for how to approach a variety of situations that might arise in your life. It helps you cultivate certain tendencies that make you and everyone around you better off. As I've argued in several books and at multiple conventions, if we pay close enough attention to *Doctor Who*, we'll see it too gives us an ethic—a prescription for how to live so as to achieve the good life.

This book is not just a book about the good life. Determining the good life requires critical self-reflection influenced by our basic understanding of reality. *Doctor Who* provides several arguments for how we should understand the good life, but this book broadens the discussion to include an examination of how *Doctor Who* creates the basic framework of reality that we use when thinking of the good life. Stated differently, *Doctor Who* influences and determines our values and systems of meaning that are then interpreted into a consistent understanding of the good life.

Let's look at a couple of examples. The first step in using mathematics is learning numbers. After learning numbers, you work on mastering the concepts of addition and subtraction, and with these you have the framework to interpret the whole host of more complex mathematical equations. The appreciation of art works in a similar way. As you grow up, you're continually subjected to examples of art. Each time you engage art, whether colors, shapes, or something else, your understanding of value is further developed. You then use this understanding to interpret future experiences of art. The experiences you have early on will influence how you interpret future experiences. So, if you grow up subjected to abstract works of art, and you appreciate them, you will more than likely gravitate towards abstract works of art when you get older. This doesn't mean that you won't enjoy art that provides accurate representations of objects, it's just that your values for judging art will always filter through your value system that rank abstract art higher. This is exactly what happens when someone asks you, "Who is your favorite Doctor?" For most people, their Doctor is the first one they experienced. The first Doctor you watched creates the interpretive framework for judging every other Doctor. For me, my first Doctor was the Fourth Doctor, and as a result, my framework for interpreting reality says that the Doctor is the Fourth Doctor. So, all new experiences with new Doctors is valued in relation to the Fourth Doctor. Whether a new Doctor or new pizza, our minds constantly engage in this process of adaptation, and it can be a rather fun process, if you're aware and embrace it. My hope is that this book will help you do both.

I

Following the Doctor

1
Engaging Life Like the Doctor

It was a better life. I don't mean all the travelling and seeing aliens and spaceships and things. That don't matter. The Doctor showed me a better way of living your life . . . You don't just give up. You don't just let things happen. You make a stand. You say "No." You have the guts to do what's right when everyone else just runs away . . .

—ROSE, "The Parting of the Ways," 2005

When you're a kid they tell you it's all . . . grow up, get a job, get a house, have a kid, and that's it. But the truth is: the world is so much stranger than that. It's so much darker . . . and so much madder . . . and so much *better*.

—ELTON POPE, "Love and Monsters," 2006

To some, the Doctor is simply a wandering vagabond with a group of companions, stumbling around the galaxy and having adventures that usually involve saving a species, a planet, and occasionally, the entire Universe.

I held a similar view when I began watching *Doctor Who* in the early 1980s, and must admit, it remains a driving force behind what keeps me coming back for more. The adventures, the unknown, and the spectacle are all important parts of *Doctor Who*, but as Rose and Elton suggest in the passages quoted above, *Doctor Who* is about so much more. The Doctor teaches a way of life. In everything zie does, the Doctor engages the deep recesses of what it means to be human, and as a result, we become absorbed in the lessons of life and reality.

The Doctor teaches that we should recognize our own moral worth and the moral worth of others, for this centers our sense of self, ensuring we treat others with respect and respond appropriately when someone disrespects others or us. The Doctor, however, doesn't merely provide us with a theoretical way of structuring our lives and send us alone on our journey. That would be like giving you a key to the TARDIS and saying, "Have fun and don't get into any trouble!" Instead, zie invites us to become companions on zirs journey of self-discovery and enlightenment. Just like zirs television companions, we strive and grow from watching the Doctor and encountering the people and places zie visits. This chapter begins by describing how this process works, from our psychological engagement with watching *Doctor Who* to the Doctor's most enduring lesson—how to get lost properly!

Getting lost is probably not what you expected, but as the French term 'flâneur' suggests, getting lost provides us with a more direct and intimate interpersonal experience with others and the world, and it's this sort of interpersonal engagement that's the best way to truly come to understand the symbols and meanings of people and their communities. Literally, flâneurs are people who walk around places they visit in order to engage and gain a true understanding of the symbolic meanings and beliefs of the society.

Not only do flâneurs gain a deeper understanding of the places they visit, but they also gain a better understanding of their own values and needs. The only way to determine the unique emotional, physical, and relational needs of someone else is to get to know them in such a way that we come to have a true understanding of their values, desires, hopes, and dreams. We don't gain this knowledge by remaining distant and separated. We only gain this knowledge by getting lost in the world of others and seeing how others actually perceive and understand the universe. The trick, however, is that we can only understand others after we understand ourselves. *Doctor Who* helps us do both.

Seeing Beyond the Vortex

A straight line may be the shortest distance between two points, but it is by no means the most interesting.

— THIRD DOCTOR, "Time Warrior," 1973

The first step towards knowing thyself is to learn the skill of critical thinking. Luckily, it's one of the main lessons of *Doctor Who*.

Critical thinking can be approached in a number of ways. First, it can be viewed as a technique to be employed when performing a certain task. For instance, imagine you're in the episode "Blink" (2007), and a weeping angel has transported you to the past *with* the TARDIS. Without the Doctor's knowledge of "Timey Wimey, Wibbly Wobbly . . . stuff," it's up to you to figure out how to fly the TARDIS back to the Doctor. After your initial shock, you would need to use your critical thinking skills to solve the problem. You might try learning how to fly the TARDIS, or maybe you use your knowledge of the past to make contact with a different incarnation of the Doctor. Either way, you need to identify your problem, then work on creating a solution. In "Blink," the Doctor works with others trapped in the past to hide a series of "Easter eggs" on a specific set of DVDs, which then helps Sally Sparrow send the TARDIS back to the 1960s. Regardless of the approach or outcome, critical thinking is the tool we use to solve the daily problems we face.

Thankfully, most of us won't be asked to solve such a difficult problem, but it still illustrates how critical thinking skills are used on an occasional basis to solve particular problems. For good or ill, the fact is, people rarely go around in a constant state of analyzing their surroundings. Instead, we often have our "auto-pilot" engaged, until we need to employ careful and explicit critical thinking to solve a problem, from working the daily *Jumble* to figuring out how to pay the bills at the end of the month.

Critical thinkers ask many questions about everything and want really clear and precise answers. When I say, "everything," I mean *everything*: God, human nature, beauty, right and wrong, the inner workings of science, logic, mathematics, the nature of reality beyond human experience, personal identity, and among many other things, how humans can have knowledge of any of these things. They are much like scientists looking for the best possible explanations based on what is possible to know. In fact, until the nineteenth century, what we call "scientists" were called "natural philosophers," because they were philosophers engaged in explaining nature—the natural world. Anyone who has paid attention to some of the Doctor's scientific explanations, read a book on physics, or taken a course on theoretical physics knows that science has a way of being more akin to philosophy than what many would call traditional empirical science. Regardless of the name we give different fields of study, the hallmark of all fields of study is critical thinking.

The Doctor uses critical thinking in every episode, but to ensure that you clearly understand the power of critical thinking, recall the Doctor's predicament in "Heaven Sent." He's stuck in a castle surrounded by water, constantly hunted by a Grim Reaper-like creature. The castle is a giant "mouse trap" designed to get the Doctor to share his knowledge of the Hybrid. He instantly begins using his critical thinking skills to search for an escape and to find out who's keeping him hostage. Like many *Doctor Who* episodes, "Heaven Sent" also invites viewers to solve the same problems. In fact, part of the fun of watching *Doctor Who* is trying to solve the problem before the Doctor reaches a solution. For this particular episode, we find that the only solution is for the Doctor to spend the next few billions of years chiseling away at the Azbantium, until he finally breaks through to Gallifrey.

A second great example comes from Season Twelve's "Kerblam!" After receiving a plea for help from the Kerblam factory, the Doctor and companions set out to find the sender and to bring an end to the "random" deaths. With all of the makings of an Agatha Christie novel, the Doctor uses critical thinking, through trial and error, to uncover the culprit. Did you solve it before she did? If so, then you have some sharp critical thinking skills.

Into the Void

We're all stories, in the end. Just make it a good one, eh?

—ELEVENTH DOCTOR, "The Big Bang," 2010

With both of our examples, we find the Doctor solving a mystery, which is the task of all critical thinkers. Whether searching for something physical, like an escape from a maze, or seeking a deeper understanding of non-physical truths about morality, God, or the meaning of the universe, critical thinkers use their wits, along with lots of experimenting with trial and error, to figure out what is true and what is false. Since we're not all calculating machines, like the Doctor, we rely on a set of mental aids to help us navigate the world and determine truth.

The most important aid is that our minds are actively engaged in interpreting the world. We're not simply computers waiting for someone to enter data or install a program. Instead, our minds are constantly combining existing information about the world with new stimuli to help us survive our day-to-day activities. Take, for instance, our ability to see the world. Your mind doesn't simply perceive the environment. Your eyes have only one small portion that is capable of producing a clear image of the environment, so they continually dart around capturing data about colors, shapes, and other information, which the mind puts together as one constant image. It's really no different from the film images we see when watching *Doctor*

Who—several images are put together and sped up, creating the appearance of movement. The world we see, then, is largely the result of our minds putting together images that present the world to us.

As a result, much of the world and its meaning is shaped (or created) by our mental engagement with the world. For those thinking, "That's obvious, tell me something I don't know," such a conclusion wasn't always so obvious. Modern philosophers, such as René Descartes and John Locke, maintained that the human brain was a passive instrument structured to allow the mind to perceive ideas—mental images—of the world. These ideas were merely the result of the body sensing certain qualities, and though Descartes and Locke had vastly different philosophical positions, they both failed to recognize the brain's role in constructing what we perceive as reality.

David Hume, writing shortly after Descartes and Locke, is considered the first to argue that the brain and mind are the same, and that the mind actively constructs information from our senses, along with ideas from our memories and imagination, into something we can understand. Hume's observations were powerful and persuasive, and were so radical at the time, that the only analogy would be like walking into the TARDIS for the first time—"It's bigger on the inside!"

For those who are skeptical of the notion that our minds create reality, the great philosopher and psychologist William James provides strong evidence for how the mind performs this task. Instead of getting bogged down in James's Pragmatism, which contains some fun arguments about squirrels, we need only to turn to *Doctor Who* to explain how it works. Like any good story, our lives center around a narrative. This narrative informs us of who we are, what we believe, and what we take to be meaningful. Our perceptual abilities are like film projections, and as we use our critical thinking to engage the world, we create a narrative, just as the writers and directors of *Doctor Who* create narratives of our favorite Time Lord. As Aristotle first explained, narratives simply contain a beginning, middle, and end. Of course, like the most complex Steven Moffat story-arc, each narrative has its own logic of questions and answers; and as we engage the world, we continually generate new questions and answers based on previous ones. Noël Carroll calls this sort of narrative logic "erotetic," in order to capture the concept of a web of questions and answers. The more complex our lives, the more complex our erotetic narrative.

The Doctor's life is unimaginably complex. Yours would be too, if you could travel through time. We occasionally see the Doctor keeping a diary, but as zie points out, after so many years, keeping track of your life gets too complicated. When you're not bound by linear time, dates lose their meaning, and your narrative becomes a jumbled mess of wibbly wobbly experiences. Somehow the Doctor is able to keep track of it all. As for us humans, we consider it a success if we can keep straight the last ten years of linear time. We use memories, trinkets, Facebook timelines, and even *Doctor Who*—ever kept track of the years by the season of *Doctor Who* that corresponds to that year?—to help structure our linear lives into a chronological order that is every bit as complex as the Doctor's in their own subjective way. Within this process of organizing our narratives, we have great flexibility in shaping our narrative.

Even if we aren't good at remembering every detail, or keeping every event in its precise chronological order, our minds are good at creating narratives. They are constantly putting together the random events that occur in our lives into easy-to-understand stories full of meaning and excitement. The stories, myths, and fictions we fill our minds with will influence how we interpret new events into our narrative. We might be feeling bad, then find a $5 bill—I'm being rewarded for helping that little old lady in the grocery store. We might be lonely, then see a stranger's smile—that person is into me; I'm not an Absorbalof!

You see, no matter how far-fetched, our brains love a good story that is meaningful and ties everything together. The writers and showrunners of *Doctor Who* know how our minds work, and so spend months and years crafting story-arcs that get us interested, keep us guessing, and eventually offer some sort of closure— bringing an end to important narratives in satisfactory ways. As a result, much of our narrative is the result of our own mind creating and (hopefully) resolving personal story-arcs.

A Complicated and Ridiculous Universe

Don't worry Ace. It's only a trap!

—Seventh Doctor, "Battlefield," 1989

Our minds aren't the only thing involved in creating reality. We are all part of a culture that exists within a society that exists during a particular time in history. Depending on when and where you were born, you're bound to have a completely different understanding of reality. Those watching *Doctor Who* in 1963, in the aftermath of World War II, have a different perspective from those watching in 2005, in the aftermath of September 11th, 2001, and the War on Terrorism. Just as learning about how the mind works was important, we also need to understand how it works in relation to our historical and cultural surroundings.

With its many tropes and memes, social media provides the easiest example of how culture shapes our perspectives. Tropes are devices and conventions that are easily recognizable, and memes use tropes to quickly capture and communicate ideas, often in humorous ways. Whether it's Kermit sipping tea, Jean-Luc Picard with his hand on his forehead, or the screaming lady with the white cat, memes use the knowledge we have about certain things to communicate some bit of information quickly and easily. Noël Carroll calls this process a "realistic heuristic," meaning, common symbols and patterns from our knowledge and understanding of the outside world are used to help us easily interpret and make sense of what we're observing.

Memes aren't the only source that utilize this process. Popular fictions like *Doctor Who*, especially with its rich history, thrive on viewers being able to quickly interpret the images and tropes used throughout the show: good vs. evil, fear of the unknown, science vs. religion, romance and love, and so on. There's a reason the Master/Missy usually wears black and the TARDIS stays in the shape of a Police Box. Writers need viewers to quickly recognize the Master/Missy as evil, unless the story calls for something else, and if the TARDIS were always something different, viewers would struggle to find and identify with the iconic blue box that is arguably more popular than the Doctor. Writers use techniques to analogize character situations to our own life-situations (feelings of otherness, our gender identity, struggles with happiness), and sometimes use an actor's real-life personae to enhance characters. It wasn't random luck that Matt Lucas was hired to play the odd-looking, comedic character Nardole.

Writers also use images that viewers will figuratively associate with other character tropes—the Doctor is a savior ("Voyage of the Damned," 2007), while the Daleks are Nazis ("Genesis of the Daleks," 1975). Writers use all of these techniques (and more) to create in viewers an interpretive back-and-forth, or dialectic, where they use their knowledge and understanding of the world to interpret *Doctor Who*, which then creates expectations about the world that they apply to their everyday experiences. It's easy for viewers to think they're merely watching a show that in its own way accurately depicts the world, but the truth is quite the opposite. Instead of the images and concepts in film accurately describing the real world, they are more often normative, telling us how the world should be. This means we're not simply watching "documentaries" about a fictional time-traveler, but we're more accurately being educated about how we should live our lives. This is why popular culture is sometimes called the great educator. Instead of being passive observers, we interpret and incorporate lessons about what's normal, good, evil, and so much more, when we watch *Doctor Who*, which then informs our reality and shapes expectations of ourselves, others, and the world.

Let's tie all of these features together with Georg Hegel's influential hypothesis about the nature of history, which will help to situate our own personal experience of culture. Hegel formulated what he called the "historical dialectic" as a means for understanding history and humanity's ability to influence historical events, and since its development, Hegel's historical dialectic has dominated much of human intellectual thinking. Simply put, history is a sort of dialogue between competing cultural forces (what he calls "theses"). The thesis of one force is challenged by the thesis of another force, which then results in a synthesis of both. The synthesis, then, is challenged by a new thesis, which results in a new synthesis. Depending on our philosophical assumptions, this process of history results in different conclusions. Hegel thought the process was tied to Spirit, while Karl Marx saw the dialectic as a materialistic process leading toward the Communist utopia—complete human freedom. For us, we need only to recognize the historical struggle of competing forces as a means of creating and shaping history. To better-understand the importance of Hegel's argument, imagine the Doctor as a force for wisdom, knowledge, liberty, and among other things, compassion. In contrast, the Daleks are a force for blind obedience, exclusion, hatred, and conquest. Since the Doctor and the Daleks never completely "exterminate" the other, a synthesis is created where the Doctor and Daleks "co-exist." This historical struggle shapes the way in which the rest of the universe understands the Daleks and the threat they impose. As the Fourth Doctor explains in "Genesis of the Daleks," "Many future worlds will become allies because of the fear of the Daleks!" The Daleks' continual struggle for domination shapes the historical dialectic of the universe by causing the Doctor and others to oppose their conquests. Apart from the fictional aspects of *Doctor Who*, the show also shapes our "real" universe. *Doctor Who*, both Classic and New, spurred a collective consciousness that made it a world-wide phenomenon, which as a result, shaped history and our understanding of existence. As *Doctor Who* engages the world with episodes, books, and more, it continues to shape how history progresses.

A careful watcher of *Doctor Who* will see the historical effects of the Doctor's engagement with the world, both on television and in real life. Whether fighting Daleks, Cybermen, the Master, or everything in between, the Doctor engages and so shapes reality. If zie simply stayed on Gallifrey, or in the junkyard of 76 Totter's Lane, zie wouldn't have made a difference, just as if we stay in our homes and never engage the world. Like the hypothetical Doctor who never left Gallifrey, we would simply be caught up in the process of history, no different than a leaf caught in the gale of a whirlwind.

Getting Lost Properly

You can't just read the guidebook, you've got to throw yourself in! Eat the food, use the wrong verbs, get charged double and end up kissing complete strangers! Or is that just me?

—Ninth Doctor, "The Long Game," 2005

We should now have a greater understanding of how our minds work in relation to reality and the historical period in which we exist. We should also see the importance of being engaged, since it's the main factor in shaping reality and history. It makes us who we are, shapes our understanding of the world, and influences history. We, however, need guidance about how best to be engaged. If only we had some sort of universe-traveling expert. Oh wait, we do! Enter the Doctor, who gives us a fifty-plus-year example of how to be engaged.

Most viewers know that *Doctor Who* began as an educational show, but in case you didn't know: From the very beginning, the Doctor took viewers on adventures to historical places like Rome ("The Romans," 1965), the Aztec Empire ("The Aztecs," 1964), and on a journey with Marco Polo ("Marco Polo," 1964). The show wasn't merely concerned with winning over audiences with exciting stories about time travel, which it did, but on a much deeper level, it provided us with an example of someone dedicated to questioning and discovering truth, promoting consistency, and fostering integrity. *Doctor Who* did all of this by taking audiences to new places and introducing them to strange aliens. These lessons helped teach us to respect differences and appropriately adjust how we act (or react) to new surroundings and people. It taught us to be reflective about our own lives and the ways in which we use critical thinking. It taught us to be reflective about how we treat others and to be willing to change our views in light of new evidence. From Hartnell in 1963, to Whittaker in 2020, the lessons remain the same.

Look at what happens in the very first serial of *Doctor Who*, "An Unearthly Child" (1963). The Doctor ends up abducting two school teachers and taking them all over time and space. Not only do Barbara and Ian begin a fantastic journey that challenges every preconceived notion they've ever held, but it begins our journey of rethinking everything we thought we knew. Fast forward to "Spyfall" (2020), and the Doctor illustrates the power of open-mindedness and opposition to tyranny by introducing audiences to the historical importance and influence of Ada Lovelace and Noor Inayat Khan. From every adventure, companion, world, enemy, and narrow escape we become enlightened and learn more about our own lives and what it means to truly exist. For these reasons, and the many more that could be noted, the Doctor's life is best described as a flâneur.

The flâneur's life of engagement creates the possibility to meet others, stand for worthy causes, and oppose injustice. Of course, being a flâneur isn't always easy. In order to learn how to seek out and embrace the unexpected, we must become vulnerable, and becoming vulnerable means we open ourselves to pain and disappointment. Take, for instance, the previous quote from the Doctor that "You can't just read the guidebook, you've got to throw yourself in! Eat the food, use the wrong verbs, get charged double and end up kissing complete strangers!" Engagement requires we leave the safety of the known and seek the mysteries of the unknown. This can be a difficult lesson to learn, but here are some suggestions from the Doctor.

When the Doctor visits a place, zie seeks out the things intimately tied to a place's essence, those overlooked by everyone else. This venturing out allows the Doctor to find lesser-known places that are full of excitement and mystery, "unknown" treasures that change (and challenge) the way zie understands the world. Like the Doctor, it allows us to meet wise sages that challenge the reality of who we are, forgotten heroes memorialized in statues, beautiful sunsets, a nearly-erased historical tale, a forgotten gravesite, and who knows what else?! The Doctor is always open to learning something new, even when meeting new villains. For instance, when the Doctor meets The Beast in "The Satan Pit" (2006), he struggles to accept the idea that The Beast existed before time, yet he ponders the possibility and implications that The Beast is telling the truth. This type of engagement, which seeks and considers all possibilities, is the hallmark of the Doctor and being a flâneur, and it's what the Doctor teaches us to do.

Being a flâneur is similar to what happens to people who take strenuous and challenging vacations. Though exhausting, such vacations invite us to step outside of our comfort zones, loosen up, and get involved in things that we would've never thought possible. In a strange way, the Doctor's adventures through space and time are sort of zirs vacation from Gallifrey, which zie allows viewers to tag along to places beyond their imagination, to experience the marvels of the universe. There's no better flâneur than the Doctor. The earliest account we have of the Doctor is him rejecting the Time Lord's policy of non-interference, in order to be a "rogue." As a result, zie's perfectly willing to interfere in *any* situation that zie deems worthy of being interfered with. Because of zirs attitude of interference, the Doctor has saved the universe, saved Earth, and as this book suggests, shown countless real and fictional people a better way to live. For the Doctor, engaging in acts of interference is what makes life interesting and exciting. It influences and changes your beliefs and character, while at the same time influencing the beliefs and character of the society you engage. These aspects of interference exemplify what it means to be a flâneur.

The Good of Vulnerability

Just this once, everybody lives!

—NINTH DOCTOR, "The Doctor Dances," 2005

This journey isn't always easy or safe, so one of the main steps we must take in becoming a flâneur is becoming comfortable with being vulnerable. As an ethicist, much of my work centers on vulnerability. Our vulnerability to being wronged makes us susceptible to all sorts of abuse, and it's up to each of us to decide how we will respond. As a flâneur, you will be wronged and taken advantage of from time to time. *Doctor Who* is full of happy endings, but there are just as many struggles and pains that the Doctor endures to achieve the success of a happy ending—"Just this once, everybody lives!" As flâneurs, therefore, we mustn't deceive ourselves into thinking the life a flâneur is always easy— *Doctor Who* doesn't teach us such a lesson, neither does the real world.

Part of being comfortable with our own vulnerability is accepting the randomness of life. Albert Einstein longed for a world of order, where there was ultimately no randomness, and we typically desire the same. Our minds constantly try to order and categorize things. Think about the amount of time you've spent categorizing your favorite *Doctor Who* episodes, then imagine how frustrated you would be if it were completely random— stories with no clear narrative, random people as the Doctor, random appearance of Doctors, different companions, themes and so on. Every week, every minute, it's all different. Most fans struggle with the fact that not only does the premier date of *Doctor Who* change from year-to-year, and don't get fans started on the change from a Christmas Day to a New Year's Day episode. Now, try to imagine it being completely random. Changes make us mad, but complete randomness drives us crazy.

Randomness, however, is a good thing, if properly understood. Without randomness, all existence would be determined, meaning no free will, and without some sort of free will, there would be no freedom to make meaningful decisions, like to be a good person or to watch *Doctor Who*. We'd simply be stuck with our "fate." Quantum physics suggests that we exist in an indeterminate universe, which provides the conceptual space to say we have free will and our actions meaningfully contribute to history. Because we exist in a universe of random happenings, it also means it's okay to make mistakes. Our freedom gives us some control over our lives, though not total control, and though this freedom makes us vulnerable, it's a vital aspect of being a flâneur. It's a call to action, but it's also a call to humility.

So, instead of worrying over every single action we take, or the fact others might take advantage of our vulnerability, we should strive to be survivors, just like the Doctor. Even though the Doctor was forced to eradicate his own people and planet, zie never wallowed in self-pity. The Doctor kept engaging and growing until the opportunity arose where zie was able to change the past. At least at this point, we don't have the ability to change our pasts, but we do have the ability to change how we respond to the past. Friedrich Nietzsche teaches of the virtues of forgetting in learning to be a healthy person, and though we would be amiss to forget some things (such as the Eleventh Doctor's claim that he forgot how many children died as a result of him using the Moment, in "The Day of the Doctor," 2013), we must find some healthy way to move on from our mistakes and the wrongs that others commit against us. I'll look at these issues more closely in Chapter 4, but for now, the main lesson to becoming a flâneur is that accepting your own vulnerability and the randomness of life are the first steps towards relaxing and more fully enjoying the process of getting lost.

Maybe you think you're not important—but you are! According to the Doctor, *no one* is insignificant. As he says in 2010's "A Christmas Carol," "You know that in nine hundred years of time and space, I've never met anybody who wasn't important before." The Doctor is right, but it's up to each of us to recognize the importance of every moment, event, and person we encounter. When you begin living an engaged life, you begin making a difference in others' lives, and they begin making a difference in yours. Once you begin to see your influence on others, your community, and the world, you begin to see why the Doctor has never met anyone who wasn't important.

Maybe you're an introvert, and you're thinking, "I could never be like the Doctor." True, you might not ever be an extrovert like the Doctor, but you don't need to be the Doctor to flourish like the Doctor. Introverts can flourish as flâneurs too. As the Doctor teaches, you have near-infinite potential to learn and grow, to influence and change the lives of others, and to make the universe a better place. Whether we blab and entertain like an extrovert, or sit quietly listening and pondering like an introvert, we're all *affected* and *effected* by the people and places we engage. In other words, simply by existing, we both influence (to affect) and cause (to effect) other people and events, while at the same time having the same done to us. Though we often focus on a small number of "great" historical figures, *history is made by everyone who's brave enough to engage and interfere with the world in which they're lucky enough to live.* By engaging with the world we make history. When we don't interfere, we passively become part of it. If we ignore the part we play in making history, then not only do we forget how important we are, but the whole universe loses some of its unique character. The Doctor challenges us to step out of our comfort zones and embrace getting lost.

No matter our abilities, weaknesses, or skill-sets, we can all be flâneurs. Not everyone has a TARDIS, a sonic screwdriver, or multiple regenerations. Yet, we all have the power to choose to be more engaged and more willing to leave our comfort zones to be more like a flâneur. One such approach to getting lost is to use movies, television, and books. Good entertainment not only offers a spectacle, but it also offers individuals the opportunity to visit a variety of times and places, share a multitude of experiences with many diverse people and cultures, and to grow from the experience.

For some people, shows like *Doctor Who* take the place of lost friends and family, or they provide an opportunity to travel, which is beyond their physical or economic means. Really good fiction mirrors what happens to Jean-Luc Picard in the *Star Trek: The Next Generation* episode "The Inner Light," where Picard lives a life's worth of experiences—including making friends, falling in love, and having kids—in the matter of thirty minutes. Furthermore, writers like Harry Middleton suggest a similar type of travel based merely on our ability to imagine. In *The Earth Is Enough*, Middleton talks of his two uncles who, with the aid of an atlas, travel to different places and times, in order to see parts of the world they know they'll never have the opportunity to visit. Like all current attempts at time travel, this "time travel" is the result of the imagination, but it still serves to illustrate that we can be engaged flâneurs from the comfort of our homes, as long as when we engage others—whether in person, via the Internet, or by some other means—we apply the lessons we've learned.

All Good Things . . .

Books! Best weapons in the world!

—TENTH DOCTOR, "Tooth and Claw," 2006

A flâneur approaches life like a philosopher seeking truth. You don't just go around performing random acts, but instead, there's an underlying motive for your choices and actions. Flâneurs allow for random actions, but at the heart of their approach to life is a commitment to gaining a true understanding of the people and places they visit. In other words, they want to both experience the universe but also know the truth about the universe.

Similar to the Doctor, Socrates saw himself as a midwife—one concerned with the health of the soul and giving birth to good ideas. Instead of using his talents for self-gain, Socrates was what we would call a teacher, and as a teacher, he attempted to pass knowledge from one individual to another, and to help individuals understand the truth, usually via the method of critical thinking. He wasn't concerned with "winning" an argument, nor was he concerned with others agreeing with his arguments. Socrates only cared about engaging others in a dialogue, in order to gain a deeper understanding of the justified *true* beliefs about reality.

Opposed to the Master's use of rhetoric, the Doctor is a teacher like Socrates. He's a teacher because he's dedicated to truth. Even though he occasionally deceives, which he admits to, he does so to teach important lessons: as he says to Amy Pond in the 2010 episode "Flesh and Stone," "If I always told you the truth, I wouldn't need you to trust me." Of course, a skeptical reader might complain that such an explanation just shows that the Doctor is at best parentalistic, and at worst, no better than the Master. Such a complaint would be too hasty, for the Doctor isn't merely a parent who knows best, nor is he just interested in getting his own way. If we examine the Doctor's actions over the entire series we see that he's doing more than saying, "Trust me, because I know best." Instead, he's doing something much deeper—he's helping his companions (and viewers) grow and learn from their adventures.

The Doctor isn't interested in simply telling us how to live. Instead, he wants us to engage in living, and from this, arrive at a set of principles for how to properly order our life. He isn't preaching to us about how to live a certain way, he's trying to teach us a better way to live, by having us engage in actually *living*. To accomplish his task, the Doctor must sometimes withhold certain details in order to allow us to work through problems. Just like a teacher who gives you a test, asks you a series of questions, or presents you with a difficult thought experiment, the Doctor is trying to test your mastery and understanding of a certain set of material.

He's not doing it for selfish reasons. Instead, he wants you to learn and grow, to take the things you've learned and to use them to more properly govern yourself.

The lives of the Doctor and Socrates combine to exemplify the life of a flâneur. Both are engaged and dedicated to learning, self-reflection, truth, and consistency. Both promote critical thinking as a way of life, as a tool to achieve consistency and order in one's life, as a means for searching and gaining knowledge and wisdom, and as a spiritual quest for the unknown that is good.

It's easy to get caught up in one's own way of seeing things, and to try and force others to see the world exactly the same way. *Doctor Who* tries to get us to live life differently. It calls us to engage ourselves and the world around us, to change the way we see the world and the way we treat others. It makes us consider the possibility that we might achieve "the impossible." *Doctor Who* shows us that we, and the world in which we live, is larger on the inside than on the outside, and that it's this Time And Relative Dimension in *all Spaces* that makes the world so much stranger, so much darker, so much madder, and so much *better*! It's from all of this that it teaches us to strive for something greater: a life of critical thinking lived according to the good.

Doctor Who challenges us all to consider how we view our own lives, how we treat others, and how we understand what counts as truth by presenting us with philosophical case studies in the form of episodic television. It's a never-ending process. As we watch from season to season we test the Doctor's consistency. Can zie remain consistent while being forced to deal with Cybermen, Daleks, Sontarans, Ice Warriors, the Master,

Zygons, Jagrafess, the surviving brain of the villainous Time Lord Morbius, Abzorbaloffs, Sea Devils, Slitheen, Vashta Nerada, the Silence, the Weeping Angels, and the Stenza (a.k.a. Tim Shaw)?

From watching and critically engaging the Doctor's way of life, we then engage and learn whether or not our own moral beliefs are consistent. We learn and grow from this engagement, so when we're forced to deal with other people, strangers, and enemies that actually exist here on Earth, we'll know how best to act.

As illustrated in Brian Robb's insightful book *Timeless Adventures: How Doctor Who Conquered TV*, the attempt to teach the audience can be seen throughout the series, and most of the lessons are not historical, they're ethical, moral, and sometimes spiritual. It presents viewers with ways of understanding complex issues, and gives them the tools to reflect upon and arrive at consistent philosophical conclusions.

"The Green Death" (1973) teaches viewers about the importance of environmental stewardship, but it never lays down dictates for exactly how we should treat the environment.

Episodes like "The Silurians" (1970) teach viewers about co-existing with other species. "The End of the World" (2005) raises questions about justice, death, and self-importance. The 2011 two-story arc "The Almost People" and "The Rebel Flesh" challenges viewers to consider what it means to be part of the social and moral community of equals.

The continuing story arc involving the Time War, seen throughout the New series, directly engages the themes of war, violence, nonviolence, and genocide. "The Witchfinders" (2018) has the Doctor fighting against ignorance, bigotry, and hypocrisy, and the Master's speech about the Timeless Child in "Spyfall" implies retribution for the Time Lord's misdeeds.

From these and countless other examples that could be provided, *Doctor Who* is so much more than a mere science-fiction show. It's a teaching tool that's actively engaged in challenging viewers to think, consider how they would act in certain situations, and what proper course of action is best for everyone.

2
The Dangers of Being the Doctor

We shouldn't kid ourselves. Being the Doctor is dangerous, and we aren't the Doctor. Not only does the Doctor have seemingly endless regenerations, but the Doctor is also fictional. We must not, however, let the Doctor's fictional nature deter us from accepting the fact zie serves as an exemplar for how we should live.

All fiction comes from a combination of ideas from what is real, and the goal of literature, drama, and movies is to present examples of how we should live and how we should respond to particular situations. We've looked at *Doctor Who*'s lessons on such issues, but now it's time to take a step back and recognize the dangers of being the Doctor.

Virtues of Non-Interference

Time Lords profess to live according to a principle of non-interference, but as seen in countless episodes, especially from the Third Doctor's tenure, and implied by Season Twelve's "Timeless Child," it doesn't take much for them to violate it. According to the Fifth

Doctor's comments in "Frontios" (1984), there was once a time when the Time Lords intervened in troublesome situations, but such a policy is part of their distant past. Unlike the non-interference promoted by something like *Star Trek*'s Prime Directive, the Doctor's principle of *interference* promotes "getting into the thick of things." It allows for accidental visits, crash landings, accidental cultural contaminations, and of course, the purposeful stepping in and saving planets from megalomaniacs and alien invaders.

The difference between interference and non-interference illustrates two ways in which we can engage life. On the one hand, persons practice non-interference by observing life at a safe distance, from the comfortable lives and work-environments they've created for themselves. Persons who live according to non-interference take no risks, avoid all possibilities of being embarrassed or being the center of attention, and as a result, never have to face the possibility of failure. On the other hand, persons who practice interference are engaged, take chances, and risk comfort for growth. Granted, there are advantages to the former, like being relatively comfortable and not failing at some task(s), but if you live a life completely disengaged, then you've missed out on what makes living exciting. In fact, if the Doctor's lessons on interference teach us anything, those who do not engage the world around them, in some way, have *failed* at life.

We shouldn't simply discount non-interference, however, for it has its own set of virtues. Many anthropological, sociological, and psychological experiments require non-interference to keep data from becoming tainted, either from the responses of the subjects or from the researchers themselves. By not interfering, researchers get a more accurate set of data from their study group. What's more, history and global politics provide cases when it's best not to interfere, like when a distant country experiences revolution or civil war. In some instances, interference might be good, but in others, it's best avoided.

Furthermore, depending on the nature of reality, non-interference might be the safest approach to ensure we don't "mess up" the universe. For instance, imagine we're time travelers in a semi-*deterministic* universe. In other words, the universe is governed by a strict set of causal laws, but we as humans with free will can act in non-deterministic ways. If this is the nature of reality, then anything we do in the past could destroy the timeline that allows us to exist. The Twelfth Doctor faces this problem in "Under the Lake" and "Before the Flood" (2015), and with dramatic effect, we're shocked when after going to the past, the Doctor appears as a ghost in the present. So, if determinism is true, then non-interference seems to be our best option—assuming the concept of options in a deterministic universe makes sense.

For those unfamiliar with determinism, it is the (deceptively) simple claim that all events have a cause, and these causes are governed by the laws of nature. Since every event is the result of a previous cause, then determinism maintains that the universe is the way it is and can't be otherwise. In other words, the present is determined by a set of specific past events, and the events of the present will create a specific set of future events. The present is determined by the past, and it cannot be otherwise. So, if you were able to go back in time to the distant past and you changed one little thing, it would completely alter history as we know it.

We often see this view of reality referred to as the "butterfly effect," which states that if we travel to the distant past and change a single thing—in this case, killing a butterfly—the future will be irrevocably changed. Martha Jones states such a position in the 2007 episode, "Shakespeare Code":

> MARTHA JONES: But are we safe? I mean, can we move around and stuff?
>
> THE DOCTOR: Of course we can. Why not?
>
> MARTHA JONES: It's like in those films: if you step on a butterfly, you change the future of the human race.
>
> THE DOCTOR: Then, don't step on any butterflies. What have butterflies ever done to you?

Like Martha in the beginning of her adventures, those who support non-interference have determinism as a philosophical position to show why non-interference is the wisest course of action.

One final virtue of non-interference is that it protects observers from being unduly influenced by their research subjects. We might say, observers are to be "affected," not "effected" by their experience. Being influenced—in other words, affected—to some degree can't be helped, but a researcher should never be affected so much that their beliefs and values are changed—what we might call, effected. Such changes could bias the data and taint the results. So, the observer should maintain an objective position in regard to the study group, limiting all interaction that might bias his or her objectivity, which means limiting direct and meaningful contact.

The best examples of this come from anthropology, sociology, and psychology, where observers study their subjects from a safe distance. They either do not allow their presence to be known, or they limit the awareness of their presence by pretending to be part of the study group. This approach is the goal of the Time Lords, who use their TARDISes to travel, observe, and gather data. In fact, the TARDIS is the ultimate anthropological tool for observing and experimenting on other cultures: it can blend in with any environment, has infinite internal space for gathering and storing samples, a vast array of clothes, and it's connected to the Amplified Panatropic Computer Network linked to the Matrix, which collects and stores all of Time Lord's and TARDIS's data and experiences for future study. The Doctor attempts such an approach in "The Fires of Pompeii" (2008). Of course, he fails. Despite his attempt to be an objective observer, he finds that in order to save the world he must make Mount Vesuvius erupt and destroy Pompeii. More importantly, Donna convinces him to subjectively engage by saving Caecilius and his family, ultimately taking on his appearance to remind him to save people, no matter the consequences. In other words, he starts the adventure with the goal of being affected, but ends up being effected, which leads to effecting the lives of Caecilius, his family, and those they then effect in the future.

With the above virtues in mind, the ideal of non-interference is to be an objective observer, and objective observers are *affected* but not *effected* by their subjects. As the opposite of being a flâneur, objective observers are influenced by what they see, but are not changed in the deep and meaningful way people are changed when they engage in intimate personal relationships. The data collection process might change the way the observer acts or thinks, but only in a limited, disconnected way. There's never any "real" interaction between observer and observed, as would occur if a person were to immerse themselves in an environment, take part in its rituals, and interfere with the locals.

Non-interference influences how individuals perceive themselves and how they understand the world around them, and it suggests a way of life that is disengaged and separated from interacting with the world and others. As a result, non-interfering objective observers often miss the deep-rooted meanings behind and within the observed society, which also means they add nothing to and gain very little from their experiences.

What Dignity?

Some readers might prefer non-interference because it seems easier, but is it truly the best way to live? Virtues are supposed to promote individual flourishing and communal justice, and a life of non-interference risks letting others suffer and threatens to inhibit flourishing. If non-interference is going to work as a way of life, then we must ensure that non-interference respects human dignity. But what is 'dignity'?

Terrence Des Pres claims in *The Survivor* that dignity no longer means much in analytical discourse, but it remains a powerful concept in protecting individuals from wrongdoing. Think about Karl from "The Woman Who Fell to Earth" (2018), who underestimates his worth and listens to self-motivation messages to help recognize his own dignity. The message is easily missed, but the whole reason the Thirteenth Doctor battles "Tim Shaw" (Tzim-Sha) is to protect the dignity of people like Karl. The Thirteenth Doctor's adventures highlight the importance of "the Fam" and how all share a sense of dignity, no matter their "handicap," difference, or weakness.

According to Des Pres, dignity is an "inward resistance" to being dominated, "a sense of innocence and worth, something felt to be inviolate, autonomous and untouchable, and which is most vigorous when most threatened," and an "irreducible element . . . of selfhood . . . whose function is to insist upon the recognition of itself *as such*." Stated differently, instead of dignity being some mystical feature that somehow makes one better than others, dignity is the basic worth of beings that protects them from being enslaved and wronged by others. Dignity, then, is a fundamental feature of our humanness that exists as the foundation of our individual engagement with others in various communities, and we should embrace its use in protecting ourselves and others.

From space adventurers to Rosa Parks, and factory workers to sentient universes, the Doctor is unable to sit back and allow others to be wronged. For the Doctor, non-interference allows children to cry, evil to conquer, and the destruction of worlds. Non-interference might recognize dignity, but it doesn't protect and promote dignity. The only way to protect and promote dignity is to actively engage, and with some help from friends, succeed in ensuring the dignity of all.

Maybe you think we shouldn't trust the example of a fictional alien. If so, here are two examples from real life.

Adam Michnik spent several years of his life in prison for critiquing the communist regime in Poland. Though mistreated and held against his will, he produced some of the most thoughtful works on living an engaged life. In fact, he wrote five books while in jail! In Adam Michnik's view, we must never give up, for positive change depends on a sustained personal and political dignity. Such dignity recognizes the frailty of all humans, and so looks for ways to compromise, in order to achieve peace.

We can't simply be closed-minded Daleks looking to destroy, or the Master seeking revenge. Instead, we must navigate the difficult aspects of life, recognizing the vulnerability of all people, strive to find innovative ways to coexist, and at times suffer and die for what is right. Michnik survived his ordeal, and after eventually getting the opportunity to talk with the person responsible for his imprisonment, found his "enemy" to be a fragile human person just like himself, capable of truth, honesty, and compassion.

The second example comes from Václav Havel, the persecuted Czech dissident who became president of Czechoslovakia, who develops what he calls the "power of the powerless" to explain our struggle to engage within a world that is often all-too-hostile. For Havel, we all have existential pressures and vulnerabilities that keep us in a constant state of fear—fear of losing our individuality by being denied the things that make us who we are. Havel gives us the example of a storeowner who lives in fear of being oppressed by the people and his government, so he supports the government he hates, in order to remain a storeowner. The storeowner was unwilling to stand by his moral convictions, and so promoted the power that keeps him powerless.

To use an example more easily understood, imagine if you lived in a state where if you disagreed with the ruling government, they would take away and deny you any old or new *Doctor Who*. Do you support the government to save your *Who*, or do you defy them, and risk losing it all? Similar to Michnik, Havel tells us to find ways to overcome our fears. We must resist by creating parallel structures of resistance. We use our powerlessness to remain true to our identity and find ways of retaining our dignity through resistance. In "Rosa" (2018), we find the example of Rosa Parks living out this philosophy of dignified engagement. Parks did not compromise her place on the bus, Martin Luther King, Jr. did not compromise his march to Selma, Alabama, and Jesus of Nazareth did not compromise his place on the cross. These are all cases of dignified action that required different sorts of sacrifice, but that respected and protected the dignity of all, which wouldn't have occurred without a policy of interference.

To Be Compassionate Is to Be Vulnerable

The greatest fears of an engaged life are failure, death, and the existential vulnerabilities that both engender. *Doctor Who* doesn't suggest that such a life is easy, but it does show that living such a life is possible. In "The Woman Who Fell to Earth," Gracie dies, Ryan loses his Nan, Graham loses his wife, yet they all gain a family. Sure, along with Yaz, they all wind up in the vacuum of space, but eventually they find themselves safe and enjoying the adventure of their lives.

In the face of loss and death, the Doctor's approach is: "Sometimes I see things need fixin'," and she does what she can to fix them. In "Stolen Earth" and "Journey's End" (2008), the Daleks name him "The destroyer of worlds," and mock him for his compassion. After the TARDIS is supposedly destroyed with Donna inside, the Supreme Dalek taunts, "If emotions are so important, surely we have enhanced you?" Yes, the Doctor feels pain, but this pain is proof that people are important. We don't feel pain and sorrow for things of which we don't care. Our pain affirms the importance and dignity of others, and so it is normal that we still fear the pain and vulnerability of caring and recognizing the worth of others.

Therefore, we shouldn't reject these fears and vulnerabilities. As Clara expertly explains in "Listen" (2014), it's fear that makes us kind. Even in the face of death, the Tenth Doctor shows compassion for the Master ("Last of the Time Lords," 2007). In "Earthshock" (1982) emotions enhance life; ". . . small beautiful events are what life is all about." Instead of making weapons, we should make shields for those who have been wronged, and that even when our adversaries tell us that compassion is the greatest weakness (Davros in "The Witch's Familiar" 2015), we respond like the Doctor, saying, "I wouldn't die of anything else." When we approach life in this way, we might feel lonely like the Doctor, but as Sarah Jane notes in "Journey's End" and the Thirteenth Doctor's traveling companions show, we gain a family—a family of all people who recognize dignity in others and strive to ensure their protection.

A Little Real-Life Help

Maybe you're still skeptical, thinking, "That's all well and good for the Doctor, but I'm introverted, I'm shy, I'm scared, or simply, I can't do that!" These are all good points, and as we just discussed, they're all perfectly natural human responses. *Doctor Who*, however, teaches us that anyone can be fantastic. It takes work, and involves failure, but the Doctor thinks that all—except maybe "pudding brains"—can achieve it. What if the Doctor is wrong? What if it's not just pudding brains who can't be fantastic? What if the Doctor's engaged way of life is simply too demanding?

In ethics, if a theory is too demanding, then it's rejected as an inadequate theory. Is the Doctor's ethic too demanding? First, we must be able to admit that not all demandingness is bad. As discussed in my book *Repentance and the Right to Forgiveness*, moral egoism ("do whatever one desires") makes no demands of agents. This complete lack of demandingness suggests moral egoism is no moral theory at all, because it allows all actions, including those that wrong others.

The hallmark of generally accepted moral theories is that they call on agents to perform certain actions based on a consistent set of reasons inferred from a basic assumption of value. As a result, moral theories often demand we do (sometimes difficult) things that run counter to our desires. The Doctor is often scared, yet zie resists the temptations to let evil win. As mentioned previously, this internal resistance is dignity. Of course, we shouldn't always act exactly like the Doctor, since we aren't Time Lords with multiple regenerations. So, our initial skepticism of living like the Doctor has merit, but our meaningful, inward resistance will be determined by the specifics of our particular lives. Resistance-as-engagement against those who disrespect dignity can appear in the form of a disapproving glare, a quiet conversation with other individuals about how it is wrong to harm others, or even a well-intended social media post.

Doctor Who teaches viewers that proper engagement and resistance to wrongdoing is contextual to our lives, but also challenges us to understand and strive to meet the standards of other ethical contexts. Our morals and willingness to engage develops within particular times and communities, just as our love for particular Doctors and episodes is dependent on when and where we are reared. As William Sim discusses in "Internalization and Moral Demands," each community develops and internalizes their own set of moral standards, and as a result, outsiders perceive certain moral demands as too great, while members of the particular moral community view the same demands as no greater than any other basic moral demand. The Doctor sees combating Daleks, Cybermen, and Universes as part of zirs minimum moral requirements, while we humans see such tasks as beyond our limited abilities. To quote the Sixth Doctor, "Unless we are prepared to sacrifice our lives for the good of all, then evil and anarchy will spread like the plague . . ." ("The Trial of a Time Lord," 1986). That sounds great if you can regenerate, but is it too demanding for humans?

To answer this question, we need look no further than the French village of Le Chambon. The population of Le Chambon were "normal" humans living according to what they perceived as an "easy" moral demand— love one another, and to love one another meant they refused to turn neighbors over to the Nazis and other collaborators. Simple, right? Yet we often still look at the command to love one another as something that is too demanding. Yet, the example of the people of Le

Chambon standing up to the Nazis simply by saying 'No' to soldiers seeking Jewish refugees, and being successful, shows that the demandingness of doing what is right is often much easier than we expect. It's definitely scary, and *Doctor Who* does a nice job of showing how scary it can be to be engaged. Yet, it also shows how when we exhibit the courage of standing up to evil, we gain companions on our journey.

The people of Le Chambon were successful because they worked together as a community. If some members of a society exhibit a willingness and capacity to resist, then other members will join the struggle. Martha Jones creates such a resistance movement in "The Last Time Lord," when she traveled the planet telling people of the Doctor. When they all thought of the Doctor, he was then able to defeat the Master. The same is true in "The Lie of the Land" (2017), when humanity overthrows The Monks oppressive control. So, yes, we might sometimes be limited by what we think is possible when ethics demands our action, but even in the face of great fear, *Doctor Who* teaches us to join with others in an attempt to create a united front against wrongdoing that helps us overcome our fears and shortcomings.

Once we recognize our limits and fears, then start working with others to insure all are treated justly, we create the "parallel structures" of resistance that Havel suggests give power to the powerless. As individuals we can't be expected to fix every injustice, but ethics requires that we respond in some way. Even if you're only comfortable taking the approach of an objective observer, you're still responsible for how you contribute to injustice. So, you must insure that the ways in which you do use your time, energy, and money promote justice. Being a disengaged objective observer doesn't give you permission to act unethically, whether by purchasing clothes made in sweatshops or bullying people from fake social media accounts.

Doctor Who, on the other hand, recognizes our human tendency to separate and live the life of an objective observer. Yet, it calls on us to be more, to be engaged, to be fantastic. Like Iris Young proclaims, the Doctor teaches that no matter one's position within a community, one has certain moral responsibilities to discharge, and the best way to carry out this responsibility is to live an engaged life helping others. It can be a difficult and scary approach because we are so vulnerable, but these same "shortcomings" are why such a life promotes the flourishing of all individuals and communities. Like Martha Jones, we should be careful to avoid causing unnecessary harm, like killing butterflies, but if we are to truly live and be fantastic, we must risk the comfort of being disengaged. We can recognize and enjoy the virtues of non-interference when it's appropriate, but the risk to human dignity is too great for us to live a life dedicated to non-interference. Instead, we must self-reflect and discover our own strengths and weaknesses, find ways—often with the help of others—to use our strengths to engage, and learn to embrace a life of being fantastic. Yes, there are dangers to being a flâneur like the Doctor, but the risk of not trying to live such a life is that we might find ourselves at the end of life, realizing that we never truly lived.

II

Everyday Life as the Doctor

3
What Is Who?

I know exactly who I am. I'm the Doctor.

—THIRTEENTH DOCTOR, "The Woman Who Fell to
Earth," 2018

Personal identity can be framed in two different ways, as a question of what it means to be "you" right now, or as a question of what it means to be "you" after death.

Though deceptively simple on the surface, questions of personal identity are notoriously difficult. Thankfully, there's no better companion to have on our journey to discover the truth concerning personal identity than the Doctor. In fact, besides historical analysis, personal identity is probably the most written about topic of *Doctor Who*. It's also a favorite topic of the show's writers. The Eighth Doctor's choosing to take on the identity of a War Doctor, the Tenth's and Eleventh's refusal to identify with the War Doctor, and the resulting acceptance of all these disparate personality types shows how important personal identity is to the show.

Peter Capaldi's first episode "Deep Breath" (2014) features an extended discussion of personal identity, and Ashildr/Me raises serious questions of identity and timelessness, as does Clara's Impossible Girl storyline. With extended monologues on identity and the ever-mysterious revelation of the Doctor as the Timeless Child, Jodie Whittaker's tenure has been no different.

The Wheel Weaves as the Wheel Wills

Time never stops, and whether you see it as an enemy or companion, time is something that we all must come to terms with in our lives. We can run from it, deny it, or attempt to cover it up, but time affects us all. Like a river that continually flows, we grow and age with every second, hour, week, and year; and though many have tried to dam the river of time, no human has overcome the never-ceasing change that is time. Sure, we could easily get depressed about this fact of life, but that's not what the Doctor would have us do, nor would most philosophers. Instead of running in fear, we merely need to spend some time analyzing time, in order to see that it's just one of the many challenges of life to understand and embrace.

Time creates a major problem for personal identity because time implies change. Change might not seem like that big of a problem, but it wreaks havoc on the concept of personal identity. In order for something to have a stable identity implies it has the same qualities over time. If those qualities change, then it's unclear what we mean when we say, "It's the same object." For example, you know the episode "The Woman Who Fell to Earth" by the individual scenes (the qualities) that make up the episode. If the scenes were different each time you watched the episode, it would be a different episode and you wouldn't know which episode you were watching. We need the scenes to remain the same for the name "The Woman Who Fell to Earth" to properly apply. Yet, some things change all the time and we don't necessarily think they lose their identity. Your body, for example. Even though your body constantly changes, somehow it makes sense to say it's the same body and the same "you."

This seemingly basic truth of identity is problematic because all of existence appears to be in a constant state of change. Even rocks undergo constant change from weathering and other outside forces. So, if everything is always changing, then just like our *Doctor Who* episode, we shouldn't be able to know anything about the world. Yet, we do! In fact, we're really good at recognizing the objects and people we encounter on a regular basis, even if they are technically different from our last encounter. How can this be?

Early philosophers, like Socrates and Plato, noticed these issues of identity and assumed another realm of existence, a realm of being, where the eternal, unchanging Forms of objects exist. The world in which we exist is filled with objects that represent the Forms, as imperfect copies, and it's only through rational contemplation that we come to understand the Forms and, therefore, recognize the ever-changing objects of our world. So, even though a river is always changing, we can look at the flowing body of water and accurately say "river," because our mind recognizes how it represents the Form of river. The same is true for rocks and trees, and for concepts like beauty, love, and wisdom.

In regard to the identity of individual humans, Plato thought that humans have eternal souls that exist, similar to the Forms of objects and concepts, yet often find themselves trapped in physical bodies. As a result, even though we often associate identity with a physical body, true identity is located in the soul. Without the soul, our ever-changing bodies would prevent others from accurately recognizing us; but because of our soul, there's an unchanging constant that grounds our identity and makes us recognizable. We sometimes see the suggestion of something similar in *Doctor Who*, when Time Lords recognize each other, even though they've been through multiple regenerations. Since each Time Lord looks drastically different from their past incarnation, there must be something stable that others recognize. Plato would say it's their soul.

The tension behind these issues is between being (unchanging) and becoming (changing), and it has been the focus of philosophers and theologians for many thousands of years. Until recently, very few—Heraclitus and Friedrich Nietzsche, to name two—have embraced a philosophy of becoming. As a result, we have many inventive ways for describing how we can know something, especially something like personal identity, even though it's constantly changing. Let's look at few of the explanations.

The Journey, So Far

To set the stage, observe the Thirteenth Doctor's monologue from "The Woman Who Fell to Earth":

THE DOCTOR: You should have seen me a few hours back. My whole body changed.

> Every cell in my body burning. Some of them are still at it now, reordering, regenerating. . . . There's this moment where you're sure you're about to die and then you're born. It's terrifying. Right now I'm a stranger to myself. There are echoes of who I was and a sort of call towards who I am. And I have to hold my nerve and trust all these new instincts—Shape myself towards them. I'll be fine . . . In the end . . . Hopefully . . ., I have to be, because you guys need help and if there's one thing I'm certain of, when people need help, I never refuse. Right? This is going to be fun.

Quite a bit has already been written on *Doctor Who* and personal identity. Let's start with a survey from the section on personal identity, from *Doctor Who and Philosophy: Bigger on the Inside.*

In his chapter, "Just as I Was Getting to Know Me," Patrick Stokes discusses the evolution of the Self. As we've seen, the Self was first associated with the concept of a soul, which then became associated with the physical body, thanks to philosophers like Aristotle. The Self-as-soul versus Self-as-body remained the center of debate, until René Descartes in the 1600s developed undeniable arguments for the existence of the mind, as a thinking substance (we looked at this in Chapter 1).

Descartes's argument seemed to settle the debate—the Self is the mind (soul or consciousness). One problem with Descartes's argument is that we never actually perceive a Self, nor can we find any physical evidence of its existence. In fact, real-life examples such as Phineas Gage, who survived having his brain impaled with an iron rod, which then resulted in drastic changes to his personality, suggest that personality appears to be tied to the physical brain and not a non-physical soul. To avoid this problem, John Locke argued that personal identity is found in psychological continuity over time. We remember what happened to us yesterday, so it seems that we must be the same person we were yesterday, even though we have changed.

Ah, but sometimes we change drastically, though nothing like the Doctor regenerating, and sometimes we can't remember everything from our past. In "The Timeless Children" (2020), the Doctor discovers she has lived many forgotten lifetimes, which causes her to question her identity. So, is she not the Doctor prior to the Hartnell Doctor? Am I not the same person as the five-year-old me because I don't remember anything about him? An answer of "yes" to either of these questions seems dubious, because they seem to be the "same." As a result of these and similar examples, some philosophers reject psychological continuity as an adequate theory of personal identity.

So we come back to the physical continuity of our bodies to support personal identity. The Doctor's ability to regenerate, however, undercuts the possibility of physical continuity being acceptable. Ponder the following statement from the Twelfth Doctor to the clockwork Half-Face Man:

> DOCTOR: You are a broom. Question. You take a broom, you replace the handle, and then later you replace the brush, and you do that over and over again. Is it still the same broom? Answer? No, of course it isn't. But you can still sweep the floor. Which is not strictly relevant; skip that last part. You have replaced every piece of yourself, mechanical and organic, time and time again. There's not a trace of the original you left. You probably can't even remember where you got that face from. ("Deep Breath," 2014)

Within this short speech, the Doctor has summed up the history of philosophy as it relates to personal identity, and of course, even though he appears to be talking to the Half-Face Man, he's really talking to himself. His statements are especially appropriate in light of the revelations of the Doctor as the Timeless Child.

To help with this riddle, Greg Littmann's chapter, "Who Is the Doctor? For That Matter, Who Are You?" shows how the body criterion for personal identity fails. For one, *Doctor Who* shows that it's possible to exist in a different body or even without a body. Another thing to consider is the fact that the Doctor regularly changes zirs body, yet zie is still called the Doctor. Littmann notes the two examples of how Ursula exists as a paving stone in "Love and Monsters" (2006), and Jamie McCrimmon is turned into cardboard in "The Mind Robber" (1968). If our body is essential for personal identity, then Ursula ceases to be Ursula when she becomes a paving stone, and the same is true for Jamie.

Littmann also shows how the memory requirement is problematic. First, in episodes where the Doctor meets earlier incarnations, zie should remember these previous encounters. Yet, zie doesn't, and even though the writers often cite some sort of time paradox, the Doctor not remembering zirs past suggests memories aren't what determines personal identity. Second, if memories are required, we must conclude that John Smith in "Human Nature" and "The Family of Blood" (2007) is not the Doctor, even though he shares many of the same personality traits. The final problem that Littmann notes is that episodes like "The Hand of Fear" (1976) and "Resurrection of the Daleks (1984), where villains steal the memories of other characters, doesn't change the character of the villains—Eldrad doesn't become Sarah Jane and the Daleks don't become the Doctor.

Littmann offers important help, but there are a few other options to consider. Richard Hanley offers a novel explanation in "Who's Who on Gallifrey." He suggests an approach that relies on the concept of the closest continuer. Incorporating his previous work on the theory of teleportation, as an instantaneous matter transport, Hanley suggests that what really happens during teleportation is that your "information" is stored, transferred, and constituted anew. Instead of your body moving from one tele-pad to another, the details of our mind and body are recorded, your body is destroyed, and then constructed anew with the stored information in the system. If Hanley's description of teleportation is true, then even though your transported self is brand new, it's still the closest continuer of your pre-teleported self. You're so close that you (and others) don't even recognize you're different.

He uses the example of Jackson Lake to show how Lake is a close continuer to being the Doctor, since he has the Doctor's memories, but he's not the closest, since the Doctor still exists ("The Next Doctor," 2008). The same seems to be true when we consider the Doctor's decision to save the young Amy Pond in "The Girl Who Waited" (2011). The aged Amy was still Amy, but the young Amy was the closest continuer to the Amy before entering the quarantine facility on Apalapucia. We can also look at "Hell Bent" (2015), when the Doctor has his memories of Clara erased. These were important, character-shaping memories, yet even with his memories of Clara erased, Capaldi's Doctor is the closest continuer. He continues his journey as the Doctor, just as we continue to recognize him as the Doctor.

In "Is the Doctor Still the Doctor—Am I Still Me?", David Kyle Johnson suggests four-dimensionalism as a final explanation of how we should understand personal identity. According to four-dimensionalism, a person only exists across time. If true, then trying to pinpoint any one instance of a person is impossible. Personal identity can only be determined by examining the person as a whole. When we look at individual instances of a person, we're only seeing one instance of an individual engaging in the process of being a whole person. These individual instances are called "person-stages." Based on this explanation, Johnson suggests that we understand personal identity as we do *Doctor Who*. *Doctor Who* is a television series that has many individual serials and episodes. Each episode is part of *Doctor Who*, and helps decide the identity of the entire series, but we can only determine the whole identity of the show when we no longer have stories to tell of our rogue Time Lord—hopefully never.

For Johnson, we should understand human personal identity in the same way. Our lives are the series, while our individual person-stages are the episodes. As a result, we shouldn't be surprised by how easy it is to present cases where minds and bodies are swapped, which wreak havoc on our attempt to settle on a consistent theory of personal identity. It's like watching one episode of *Doctor Who* and trying to explain the entire series.

If you watch something like "Kill the Moon" (2014), you might say that *Doctor Who* is fantasy, whereas if you watch "The Brain of Morbius" (1976), you might say it's gothic horror. Either way, it's a mistake to define *Doctor Who* according to one episode, just as it's wrong to base personal identity on one life-event. If this four-dimensionalism is true, then like the Doctor, Johnson maintains we're all wanderers in the fourth dimension.

To sum up the story so far, theories of personal identity based on bodily continuity, memories, and character traits all seem to fall short of a being satisfactory explanations. Hanley's closest continuer explanation offers hope, as does the David Lewis-inspired four-dimensionalism discussed by Johnson. These theoretical explanations are helpful, but they seem to overlook certain psychological and existential explanations that might provide more practical guidance in our everyday lives.

The New Adventures

For existentialists, personal identity is not something static. It changes along with the choices we make. You see, existentialists maintain there's no predetermined essence or soul that determines who we are, but instead, we create our essence by filling our lives with meaning from the choices we make. Whether a theist, atheist, or time-traveling alien, existentialists maintain that we have complete control over our actions, and therefore, are completely responsible for the personal identity we create in response to the world. The Doctor seems to hold this view in "The Woman Who Fell to Earth":

> We're all capable of the most incredible change. We can evolve while still staying true to who we are. We can honor who we've been and choose who we want to be next. Now's your chance. How about it? . . . Bit of adrenaline, dash of

outrage, and a hint of panic knitted my brain back together. I know exactly who I am. I'm the Doctor. Sorting out fair play throughout the universe.

Being the Doctor is a choice, and it's one in which zie delights. We, too, decide who we are based on the choices we make. Being engaged and reflecting on who we are, and who we want to be, sets the stage for how we should live our lives; and it's through living an engaged life that our personal identities become reality.

Our look at discussions of personal identity before we got to existentialism all seem to assume, like Plato, that personal identity is ultimately grounded in some sort of unchanging notion of the Self. Existentialists, and the Doctor, understand personal identity as something that is constantly becoming. There's no unchanging Self to discover. Who we are shifts constantly and evolves based on our response to external stimuli and challenges, and internal desires and calculations on how to achieve those desires. As a result, who we are is like the narrative of a book that is constantly being written. The Self, then, is like the lead actor in a story, and the decisions we make develop the plot, climax, and conclusion that is our lives.

To help understand this narrative approach, Travis Langley's and Aaron Sagers's chapter "Who's Who" in *Doctor Who Psychology* suggests understanding the Self in terms of certain character traits that exist as we live. There are cardinal traits that inform everything we do, central traits that affect most of what we do, and secondary traits that affect only part of our lives. Cardinal traits are popular in fiction, but not common in life. Take for instance the Master/Missy, who exhibits the cardinal trait of being an insane mastermind, bent on mischief, destruction, and punishing the Doctor. We get the sense that zie never takes a break or is concerned with anything other than these actions. It's easy to write a character who has cardinal traits, but the truth is, humans lack the ability to live such dedicated lives. We struggle to stay focused for fifty minutes while we watch an episode of *Doctor Who*. Instead, most people have a handful of central traits that affect most of our behavior. The Doctor is often written as a more complex character, so we have many examples of zirs central traits. The Doctor's central traits are what R. Alan Siler call the Doctor's "Magnetic North" of being a good person ("Magnetic North," in *More Doctor Who and Philosophy*) and Langley and Sagers refer to as a "steadiness under pressure, risk-taking, extraversion (outgoing), and an ego of leadership that emerges when required." These central traits are then supplemented by zirs secondary traits of having fun, reading books, listening to music, eating Jelly Babies, and of course, drinking tea. We all have similar central and secondary traits, and depending on how we live our lives, these combine to the create the story of our personal identity.

Even with the concept of character traits, there are different ways that we might try to make sense of how we create the personal identity of our Self. Friedrich Nietzsche uses what he calls the "eternal recurrence" to suggest that we approach life as though we are fated to repeat this life for all eternity. You better make this life a good one, since you'll spend eternity repeating it. Albert Camus uses the Myth of Sisyphus to implore readers to embrace to the absurdity of life and make life meaningful. In the Greek myth, Zeus punished Sisyphus to spend eternity rolling a rock up a hill, only to have it roll back down, endlessly. Camus uses the myth as an analogy of life, showing that everything we do in life is pointless and will be forgotten. If true, the natural response to the absurdity of this meaningless existence is to give up, but Camus argues that we should instead embrace the absurdity and delight in what we take to be meaningful. The writer of the Hebrew scriptural book Ecclesiastes takes a similar approach. Often attributed to Solomon, the book begins with the refrain, "Meaningless! Meaningless! . . . Utterly meaningless! Everything is meaningless." With these resounding words of "encouragement," Solomon goes on to tell readers that in the face of this meaninglessness, we should embrace God as the source of meaning, eat, drink, and be merry.

It's easy to read these authors as being depressed, but when you come to understand their true meaning, the opposite is true. As we find in Buddhist teachings, which maintain that the first Noble Truth is that "life is suffering/sorrow," it's only by accepting the impermanence and eventual destruction of all things, that we truly learn to appreciate the things that we have. Existentialists begin by recognizing that we all die, and that our lives are merely a drop of water in the ocean. As a result, it's impossible to make a quantitative mark on existence, just as one drop doesn't make a quantitative mark on the ocean. We're then left with the only option of making a qualitative difference, if we're courageous enough to live such a life. Therefore, like the Buddhist teaching, it's only by recognizing our limited existence that we gain the ability to truly exist as free beings.

Living such a life has its difficulties. It takes self-awareness and dedication, courage and resiliency, and constant perseverance; and even then, there are no guarantees in life. Much will depend on when and where we're born, our abilities, and our attitudes to the ever-changing world; but the Doctor shows us it can be done, especially if we have companions there to help us flourish. The Doctor-Companion model of *Doctor Who* presents a framework for how our personal identity is grounded in the relationships we have with those around us. We are not to be lone individuals, but we are to find companions on our journey who enhance our existence, are enhanced by ours, and together work towards helping others and allowing ourselves to be helped.

The Community of Self

The Doctor-Companion model suggests we only realize our true identities when we exist as individuals-in-relation to others. Think of what it would be like to exist without anyone else. No conversations, friends, no interactions at all. It's not even clear you would have a language, and since the words that comprise language help you structure reality, your ability to think and imagine would be severely limited. We need other people to exist, and even if we could scrape by without others, our lives would be much less enjoyable.

Doctor Who delves into this area of personal identity by showing how differently the Doctor acts when alone vs. how zie acts when traveling with companions. When alone zie becomes desensitized to the suffering of others and struggles to find the compassion that is a fundamental feature of the being the Doctor. As River Song notes, 'Doctor' is the word for healer and wise one throughout the universe ("A Good Man Goes to War," 2011). Yet, when left alone zie threatens to become judge, jury, and executioner, the destroyer of worlds, the Time Lord Victorious, or we might even say the Master.

As noted in several episodes, the Doctor and the Master had similar upbringings, yet one became a "healer," while the other became a "dominator." Though purely speculative, the main difference between the two is that the Doctor surrounds zirself with companions, while the Master always travels alone. To travel and care for others requires the vulnerability that is part of being a flâneur. Traveling alone and caring for no one keeps people from being vulnerable, which they sometimes want, but it also cuts oneself off from the valuable relationships required for human flourishing.

In his *Politics*, Aristotle says that humans are social animals, and anyone who can't live with others or doesn't need to live with others is either a beast or a god. For Aristotle, like the Doctor, flourishing is only found by having relationships with others. We need friendship, companionship, and love, all of which are part of being in a community. No matter how strange we feel, or how often we're treated as an outsider, we strive for communal interactions and acceptance. We don't always find the community in which we live supportive or capable of letting us flourishing, but this is where *Doctor Who* separates itself from most other fictional universes—it's created its own community of acceptance that grounds and provides an escape for fans.

Doctor Who's fandom began in 1963, with the airing of "The Daleks" (sometimes called "The Mutants" or "The Dead Planet"). Almost overnight, Dalekmania began, and in many ways, it's as strong today as it's ever been. Thanks in large part to the Daleks, *Doctor Who* quickly expanded into comics, commercials, variety shows, and of course, fandom conventions. *Doctor Who*'s fandom is so powerful that Trekkers have been known to make fun of Whovians for their obsession. Nevertheless, it was the dedication of Whovians after the Classic series's cancelation in 1989 that kept the show alive and inspired a new era of authors and creators to revive the show in 2005. As the series treks towards its sixtieth anniversary, the fandom remains as strong and opinionated as ever, and it's this fandom that offers an interactive community for individuals from all over the globe to participate, flourish, and develop unique personal identities. No matter how strange we might find themselves labeled at "home," Whovian fandom allows fans to find their real home and identity in *Doctor Who*.

Jean-Paul Sartre presents an insightful way for how we might understand the development of the Self in relation to our home communities and Whovian communities. Prior to Sartre, the dominate explanation for the Self came from Sigmund Freud. Freud argued that all humans have a base, animalistic drive known as the id, and that as a result of familial and societal pressures, each person develops a superego designed to keep the id in check. For instance, your id might say, "Find where your favorite Doctor lives, go to their home, try on their clothes, and take a comfy nap in their bed," while your superego steps in to say, "No, that's wrong, and you should feel ashamed for even thinking about such an invasion of privacy." From this internal struggle, Freud thought that your ego developed. Your ego, then, is the result of two competing impulses, and as a result, you're likely to have some serious psychological problems.

Sartre found Freud's argument to result from what he thought was a misguided belief in the transcendence of the ego. For Sartre, the only things we can know to exist are things that are empirically observable. The soul or Self is never empirically observable, so we can't say that it exists. Instead, Sartre shows that we can easily explain the notion of the Self in terms of our relation to others in the world. According to Sartre, each person has two identities—an external one that is simply the facts about our body (such as age and weight), and an internal one that is how we see our bodies. For most people, there's a constant tension between these two. Internally, we often see ourselves as different than our external selves.

Externally I look like a middle-aged, bearded man, while internally I see myself as a wanderer in the fourth dimension, making the world a better place by teaching and writing about philosophy. Here's where it gets really interesting. I know that my middle aged beardedness is consistent with my inner-self, but others don't know about my inner-self; so, I'm constantly trying to get others to see beyond my external realities towards my true inner-self that makes up my identity.

If I'm unable to get others to see my true self, then I'm forced into one of three choices. One, I can set myself up as an outsider, never understood or accepted. Two, I can live in Bad Faith, pretending to be someone I am not, in order to be accepted. Three, I can find a community that accepts me for who I am.

Doctor Who provides a community of acceptance for those who feel like outsiders. It provides a space for both those who live most of their lives as an outsider, and those who choose to "play the game" of being "normal." Episodes, online forums, comics, novels, blogs, and fan fiction provide an outlet for both groups, and the yearly conventions provide a space to gather, let loose, learn, and to be one's true Self. If you want to wear a three-piece suit or an elaborate cosplay, conventions let Whovians explore and discover their true identity. To use the language of Sartre, they provide a space in which our internal and external identities can come together as one, while at the same time being accepted and appreciated by others. It's within this space that we live truly authentic lives, developing an authentic identity of self.

The Doctor has a similar conversation with herself in "The Timeless Children" (2020). The Doctor seems to have no problem making zir internal self consistent with her external self. The Doctor's fashion sense suggests zie is comfortable in zir own skin, but while trapped in the Matrix, she suffers the existential crisis of discovering a forgotten past. Can she make her two identities consistent with how others see her? If not, the Master wins. Here's her moment of truth:

> DOCTOR: What are you doing here? Or are you the Matrix playing more games with me?
>
> RUTH: Don't ask me, I'm as lost as you are in here. Maybe you just summoned me.
>
> DOCTOR: Where do you fit into all this? Were you me all that time ago? Were all my memories of you erased? Did

they force me back into becoming a child? How many more of me are out there?

RUTH: I don't have those answers. But say I did, would they even help?

Doctor: Of course they would. All this, it means I'm not who I thought I was.

RUTH: Because your memories aren't compatible with what you learnt today?

Doctor: Yes.

RUTH: Have you ever been limited by who you were befoRE?

Doctor: Ah. Now, that does sound like me talking. I'm so tired! The Matrix is sapping all the energy out of me.

RUTH: No time to be tired. Still work to do out there. Lives at stake. Armies being born. People need The Doctor.

Instead of an utter collapse of identity, she realizes that being the Doctor is not a body, it's not a set of memories, it's not a theoretical proposition based on a Platonic Form, or a soul that transcends her existence. No! The Doctor's identity is what Kevin Decker calls a source of novelty created by the Doctor engaged in transforming the world. The Doctor is the Doctor because she chooses to live like the Doctor, which for us means, we too can live as the Doctor.

In *Who Is Who?*, Decker argues that humans are distinct in the sense that they "are sources of novelty and agents of transformation for their world." It's this novelty that allows us to live any way we choose. We can be fantastic, incorporating character traits of the Doctor into our own character, we can be mediocre, allowing others to decide our identity, or we can be evil, letting our inner

Master or Dalek rule. We must choose who we're going to be, and daily we must choose to craft our own identity into what we want. This is what I take to be *Doctor Who*'s most important lesson on personal identity.

A "You" that Survives Death

Personal identity deals with who we are now, but it also deals with what happens after we die. Of course, some will argue that upon death we cease to exist, but even for *Doctor Who*, such a claim is open to interpretation. For those who believe you can survive death, then we must try and determine what we mean by "you" and what part of "you" survives death.

"You" can't mean your body, since your body doesn't survive death, and if your memories are merely stored in your brain, then "you" can't be your memories either. Those who believe in a soul will argue that "you" is preserved in the soul, along with your memories and other central character traits. Of course, different religions will describe the migration of the soul in various ways, some maintaining that the soul continues to exist as a soul in some other-worldly realm, some explaining how the soul inhabits a new body in this other-worldly realm, while some suggesting that the soul returns to inhabit a new body on Earth.

Regardless of the merits of these religious explanations, the question still remains, is it still "you"? Even if I'm some sort of eternal soul, all of my identity is filtered through my human body. My desires and wants are rooted in the body, and my psychological existence is rooted in the experiences of my body in relation to the rest of existence. So, if I'm a floating soul without a body in some other-worldly realm, I seem to lose a central component of what it means to be me.

The problem only gets worse if we postulate that the other-worldly realm is a type of paradise, free from the strife and other shortcomings of our earthly existence. Many find the possibility of such a paradise reassuring, but as a philosopher, it merely raises more questions. To be human implies the existence of human character traits, such as greed, envy, selfishness, love, compassion, etc. If we get rid of all of these human character traits, then it appears that we cease to be human. If to be in paradise means we lack basic human character traits, and all we do is sit around pondering ultimate truth, then it appears that the Talking Heads were right when they sang: "Heaven is a place, a place where nothing happens." Nothing would happen because we would lack the desires required for action, and if it's a place that's perfect, we can't change—since to change implies imperfection.

One possible solution is to suggest that instead of getting rid of our human character traits, we gain the ability to better control our traits. So, we might still feel jealously, but in this paradise, we gain the willpower to not act on these feelings. I find this possibility an appealing explanation, but *Doctor Who* seems to warn against such a transformation. Both Rose ("The Parting of the Ways," 2005) and the Doctor-Donna ("Journey's End," 2008) provide examples of humans who have gained the power to overcome their limited human capacities for action and thought. For Rose, she is only saved through the Doctor's sacrificial kiss, and for the Doctor-Donna, the Doctor blocks her memories, in order to keep her from dying. So, there's not much positive evidence for this explanation in the show.

Doctor Who does provide a fairly consistent case for how we should understand how we survive death, and it's that we don't (as subjective beings) survive death. Instead of a "you" that survives death, continuing to have similar subjective experiences, *Doctor Who* suggests that the only thing that survives is the memories of ourselves in others, exemplified in the objective existence of Time Lords preserved in the Matrix.

As discussed in the book *Time and Relative Dimensions in Faith*, *Doctor Who* consistently shows the dangers of wanting to live forever, and instead, promotes the value of an objective existence where only memories of our existence survive death. For some, the objective existence of the Matrix is no better than non-existence. However, such a sentiment seems based on our inability to adequately imagine an objective existence. Our status as subjective beings prevents us from imagining an existence where we no longer have subjective experiences. Our best attempts to do so result in something like an imagined existence of being stored on a computer or being in some sort of persistent vegetative state, where we find ourselves "trapped" and unable to have new experiences. Such imaginations are fundamentally flawed, for they assume a subjective self "trapped" in some way, not allowed to have new experiences. An objective existence maintains there is no longer an individual subjective self that is capable of being trapped.

Even though such an existence is difficult for some to accept, if it's better to exist than to not exist, and existing subjectively is undesirable, then our best option appears to be some sort of objective existence. The Matrix provides such an existence, and for Time Lords this appears to be enough.

* * * * *

So, with all of the above in mind, we're left with a rather intriguing solution about personal identity. It's wrong to think of our identity in terms of some essence that is fixed and never changes. Accepting such a view puts us in a box where we're forced into accepting paradoxical arguments concerning our body and mind. If, however, we accept the existentialists' approach that we create our identity through the choices we make, we gain the power to explain our identity in terms of the daily decisions we make. We see that our identity is in a constant state of becoming. We are travelers in the Fourth Dimension, and like *Doctor Who*, we will never be able to define our full identity until we stop having new experiences.

And though it might be comforting to think of a subjective existence after death, *Doctor Who* teaches that we should find comfort in the identity we create with every decision we make, even if memories of our objective lives is all that remains of "you" after death. At the end of the day, we must choose to be fantastic, and by making such a choice, we become like the Doctor.

4

The Good of the Doctor

> As we learn about each other, so we learn about ourselves.
>
> —First Doctor, "The Edge of Destruction," 1963

We love things that are good—good episodes of *Doctor Who*, good friends, good food, good times, and of course, living a good life. As you probably heard growing up, "Doing good is its own reward," and no matter how annoyed you might have been when an adult said this to you, it's true: doing good by definition is good, and since we all like things that are good, we reward ourselves simply by doing good.

What rubs us the wrong way about the phrase "doing good is its own reward," is that there are different senses in which we use the word 'good', and so the statement seems false when doing good is difficult or painful. Yet, if we watch *Doctor Who*, we know both how difficult and rewarding it is to do good.

What makes an episode of *Doctor Who* good is different from what makes food good. A good episode requires some combination of good writing, acting, directing, lighting, and many more things. Good food, for instance good pizza, requires some combination of good crust, sauce, cheese, and toppings. No matter how much we wish it to be true, good crust and cheese do not make a good episode of *Doctor Who*! So, to understand the Doctor's lessons on the good, we need to unpack the nuances of how the word 'good' is used in different settings. Just like your typical Steven Moffat story-arc, examining the good has many twists and turns, but if we take the time to make sense of it all, we're rewarded with an extremely pleasurable, and good, experience.

Relative and Subjective Goods

The term 'good' is relative to the subject to which it is applied. If the subject of our sentence is pizza, then when we say, "That's a good pizza," we're claiming that the pizza we're referencing meets or exceeds the standards of being a pizza. If the subject of our sentence is an episode or season of *Doctor Who*, then when we say, "That's a good season," we're claiming that the season meets or exceeds the standards of a good season of television and *Doctor Who*. The word 'good', therefore, doesn't have just one set of standards, but when used in a sentence, 'good' references the standards that apply to whatever we're discussing. As a result, 'good' is relative to the subject to which it's applied.

Here's where it gets a little tricky. Not every subject has a specific and definite set of standards! Sure, moldy dough and rancid sauce might fall outside the boundaries of good pizza, but the values that contribute to determining what makes good pizza can vary substantially. Some New Yorkers reject Chicago-style pizza, claiming it doesn't meet the appropriate standards. Others reject designer pizzas from California, Hawaii, and even Canada, which is credited with creating sushi pizza. As a result, the standards of what makes a good pizza is subjective to each individual and their specific tastes, which means in these sorts of cases, 'good' is both relative to the subject and subjective to the person using the term.

Not all standards are as subjective as pizza, yet they are often used subjectively by people claiming something is good (or bad). When I say, "Season Eleven of *Doctor Who*, Jodi Whittaker's first season, is good," I mean it meets the standards I assume are required for a good season, and since I'm not a professional television writer or producer, my values of what make a good season are mostly subjective. In other words, I have certain standards I value relative to *Doctor Who*, and because I'm the sole determiner of these values, they're purely subjective to my own tastes. As a result, I can justifiably believe that Colin Baker's "The Twin Dilemma" (1984) is a good serial, and I do, even though most other people fail to see its merits.

Things would be different, if I were a professional screenwriter or television producer, though only to a degree. Professionals are trained in the specifics of what make good television. They have formulas and metrics for writing, filming, producing, and all sorts of other things of which viewers are ignorant, and even though the standards for good television evolve with new technologies and approaches to filmmaking, they create an objective way to measure whether a show or season is good or bad. So, when professionals say, "Season Eleven of *Doctor Who* is good" it has more objective weight than when I claim it is good. Of course, the opposite is also true. Many fans have said, "The writing was awful for Season Eleven," yet as non-professional television writers, what they're really saying is "Season Eleven didn't meet my subjective standards of what makes for a good season of *Doctor Who*." So, the next time you get in a heated argument over an episode or season, remember that your opinion is just as strong as theirs, unless maybe you're talking to a professional television writer.

Finally, there are certain standards of the good that prevent the possibility of any subjective interpretation. If we're talking about a good math problem, there's no room for interpreting what is meant by 'good'. Either 2 + 2 equals 4 or it doesn't. A good math problem is an equation that produces correct results, and though you might say math is bad (or evil), you're not saying that 2 + 2 doesn't equal 4. Instead, you're saying you don't like math, which has nothing to do with math, except that you find it distasteful.

The Good and the Beautiful

A discussion of taste leads us to a discussion of aesthetics. Aesthetics is the philosophical study of beauty, and besides mathematics, the examples given above all deal with aesthetics. Anytime 'good' is used to describe something we like, enjoy, or find pleasurable, we're talking about aesthetics.

Early philosophers, like Pythagoras and Socrates, worried that if "beauty is in the eye of the beholder" were true, then the concept of beauty would lose all meaning. Stated differently, if each person gets to decide the definition of 'beauty', then there's no one true definition of 'beauty'. It's whatever we decide at the moment. So, Pythagoras and Socrates argued for a rational basis of beauty, one that sees beauty as a matter of rational judgments. Humans are beautiful if they have a certain type of facial symmetry. Think of the glorious Greek statues, where each person is represented in perfect proportion and symmetry. They were able to produce such works of art because they had a mathematical formula for proper proportion and symmetry. Contemporary rationalists use what they call the Golden Ratio to discuss the beauty and symmetry of humans. If we apply this rationalist thinking to an episode of *Doctor Who*, then we can easily arrive at a set of rational objective standards that help us judge whether it's good. If the entire episode were out of focus, important lines omitted, or lacking any sort of direction, we can objectively say it's a bad episode. The problem, however, is that much more than technical features go into determining whether an episode is good.

Many Classic Who episodes contain technical issues, like wobbly sets and less-than-inspiring monsters, yet they are really good episodes. Fast-forward to New Who, where technical issues are rare, and you still have debate over the merits of episodes and seasons. For instance, most fans agree that Neil Gaiman's 2011 episode "The Doctor's Wife" is a good, but disagree over the merits of his 2013 episode "Nightmare in Silver." These sorts of disagreements appear to be based merely on personal preference, not any objective criteria. Fans will point to all sorts of "evidence" to support their position as being objective truth, but if the standard of objective beauty is technical proficiency, then both episodes are good.

In the eighteenth century, philosophers developed a theory of taste that serves as the basis for contemporary aesthetic arguments for beauty being in the eye of the beholder. Philosophers like David Hume and Immanuel Kant argued that instead of the mind making rational judgments about objects being beautiful, we *taste* their beauty *immediately*, simply by perceiving the objects. In other words, if I take a bite of sushi pizza, the tastes on my tongue will immediately determine whether I like or dislike it. I don't need to ponder whether the tastes match my intellectual concepts of good pizza and sushi. Even though we sometimes use our intellect when eating or watching something new, it's not required. We simply need to perceive an object to know whether we like it or not.

Due to the nature of perception, we typically use a mixture of both approaches. For instance, in "Beauty Is Not in the Eye-Stalk of the Beholder," featured in *Doctor Who and Philosophy: Bigger on the Inside*, Clive Cazeaux illustrates nicely the difficulty of discussing beauty within *Doctor Who*. As Cazeaux notes, there's a certain beauty of the Daleks that we immediately perceive. Their domed heads, curved roundels, and stalks are intriguingly pleasing to the eye. Yet, when looking at Daleks we can't help but recall their history of monstrous evil. As a result, our minds tend to struggle with how to categorize their beauty, because their beauty and badness conflict. A more humorous example comes from William Steig's *Shrek!*, where Shrek finds pleasurable the stench of skunks. The stench of skunks seems inconsistent with the concept of beautiful smells, which is analogous to the beauty and evil of the Daleks.

Like Cazeaux, I will leave this issue for you to decide, but it serves as a nice place to transition into our second sense of good—ethical goodness. The lesson, so far, is that the goodness of fish fingers and custard is based solely on your subjective tastes, and unless you physically force or coerce your friends into eating your concoction, it remains a matter of aesthetic goodness. However, once you bring the harm and welfare of others into the scenario, 'good' means something else. We move from aesthetics to ethics.

The Good and the Right

Morals are simply our subjective beliefs about good and bad, or more accurately, right and wrong, while ethics is the careful analysis and justification of morality—in other words, proving such beliefs right or wrong. Moral philosophers, usually called ethicists, are careful when using terms like 'good' and 'bad', because such terms are commonly associated with pleasure (good) and pain (bad), or confused with aesthetics. Because of these sorts of ambiguities, ethicists will often use 'right' and 'wrong' when talking of ethics. We'll use them both, except when it's important to make a distinction between the two.

We all have beliefs about what's wrong and right, and in fact, it's quite common to hear someone say something like, "There's no wrong or right, because we all have different opinions." For ethicists, this statement is simply false, for the straightforward reason that just because we disagree, it doesn't mean that there is no truth. Even ethicists who claim there are no moral truths beyond cultural conventions and personal subjective feelings, will often use language and cultural conventions to ground some sort of contextual moral truth. If you've watched much *Doctor Who*, you know that the Doctor believes there's a wrong and a right that applies to every being in the universe. So, for the Doctor there is moral truth. What is more, since the Doctor continually holds other beings to a moral standard, it's safe to assume that zie believes there's some sort of ethical system that ties all of our moral beliefs together. That's what we want to find and examine.

Before starting, and to help clear up any confusion, let me make some clarifying statements. First, the term 'theory' in 'ethical theory' is used in a technical sense, not in the "loosey goosey" sense used by some to mean "what I think" or "my gut feeling." For instance, I might claim to have a "theory" about who will be the next Doctor. I might even come up with some fancy explanation for how I arrived at my "theory." No matter how knowledgeable I am of *Doctor Who*, such a claim is just mere conjecture, and isn't the way ethicists (or scientists) use the term 'theory'. Compare my claim about the next Doctor to the "theory of gravity." Even though there's a lot we don't know about gravity, our theory is pretty darned consistent. If you drop an object, no matter its weight, it'll drop at a crisp 9.8 m/s^2—unless acted on by an outside force, of course. Ethical *theories* attempt to provide the same sort of consistent justification as scientific *theories*. They might not be perfect, and there's still work to be done, but contrary to popular opinion, most ethical theories do a nice job of consistently explaining many of our moral intuitions.

Unlike scientific theories that rely on observable data, ethical theories typically deal with the unobservable. For instance, when you, the Master, shrink someone to death with your Tissue Compression Eliminator, the observable data is that they were shrunk. Ethicists, on the other hand, aren't interested in the fact a person was shrunk. They're interested in what *should* have happened. For example, a typical ethicist would say "They should not have been shrunk," but to say such a thing is to say, "What occurred in the world *should* not have occurred; the world *should* be different." This is what ethicists call a "normative" claim, which is easy to spot due to the use of the word 'should', or sometimes 'ought'. Normative words like 'should' and 'ought' recognize the world is one way, but suggest it should be different. Ethical theories combine descriptive and normative claims to create arguments for how the world should be. The more complete and consistent the explanation, the stronger the ethical theory.

The second feature of ethics readers should understand is that disagreements between competing ethical theories is usually the result of what each theory values. All ethical theories use some account of *value* to distinguish what's good and right, from what's bad and wrong. Once an ethicist determines what is morally valuable, they then construct a consistent set of moral guidelines based on language, thought experiments, and the conceptual analysis of moral issues to arrive at a justified ethical theory.

Contrary to popular opinion, which would have you believe there are an infinite amount of ethical values, there are in reality only a few.

A Life of Pleasure

Developed by Jeremy Bentham and John Stuart Mill, and prominently supported by present-day philosophers like Peter Singer, utilitarianism maintains that what's morally right is that which produces the most pleasure over pain, all things considered. In other words, utilitarianism values pleasure, and when faced with a decision of how to act in a particular situation or set of situations, a utilitarian will choose the course of action that produces the most pleasure for the most people, while at the same time minimizing the amount of pain produced, for all those affected by the act. A good example of this occurs in "Genesis of the Daleks" (1975), where Sarah Jane Smith uses consequentialist reasoning to argue that the Doctor should, in fact, eradicate the Daleks, saying: "Think of all the suffering there will be if you don't [kill the Daleks]."

The Doctor, even though he eventually rejects such arguments, considers the possible consequences, and suggests Sarah Jane's calculations might be wrong; that the Daleks might actually bring about more pleasure than pain. In fact, throughout the Classic and New series, the Doctor rejects utilitarianism: zie continually stands up for the *rights* of others, making sure they get what they deserve, and forces individuals to make painful decisions in order to grow, when other good options seemed available. Watch "Kill the Moon" (2014) or "Ghost Light" (1989) for two examples when the Doctor teaches his companions a tough lesson, when he could have easily solved the problem with a lot less pain.

A Life of Duty

A life of duty is commonly referred to as duty ethics, and is most prominently associated with Immanuel Kant. As the name suggests, duty ethics is based on a notion of moral duties, grounded in the inherent worth of rational autonomous agents. Unlike utilitarianism, duty ethics doesn't care about consequences. Duty ethics seeks to determine what sort of duties a rational moral agent has to other moral agents. As a result, duty ethics values the rational abilities (or capacities) of individuals. If an individual is rationally autonomous, which means they're capable of rationally governing themselves (or at a minimum, have the potential of rational autonomy), then they have inherent moral worth.

To help illustrate, imagine the following. You're a security guard at a warehouse that just happens to be storing all of Van Gogh's original artwork. One night the Daleks attack the warehouse, setting it ablaze— "Van Gogh is an enemy of the Daleks!!!" You run to save the art, but when you get to the crate, you find a homeless person unconscious on the floor. You can only save one, so which do you save? For utilitarians, Van Gogh's artwork has more value than a homeless person, since millions of people will be saddened by the loss of Van Gogh's original art versus the relatively few affected by the loss of a single homeless person. (Nothing against homeless people. Heck, I was once homeless. If you like, imagine it's a philosophy teacher.) As a result, Van Gogh wins—In your face, Daleks! A duty ethicist, on the other hand, would say that you have a duty to save the homeless person, since they're a person with inherent moral worth. Art has no moral worth because it has no ability to be rational. It's just a thing. So, the Daleks win, but you've saved the morally worthy being.

The Doctor seems to support some form of duty ethics. As he proclaims in "A Christmas Carol" (2010), "Nine hundred years of time and space, and I've never met anyone who wasn't important." The Doctor's use of 'important' signifies his understanding of the inherent worth of all beings, even enemies. At the end of "Journey's End" (2008), he desperately tries to save his arch-enemy Davros. He also tries to save his arch-nemesis the Master in "Last of the Time Lords" (2007) and dedicates himself to reforming Missy throughout Season Ten.

Of course, there's evidence that the Doctor values more than rational autonomy, which suggests zie's not simply a duty ethicist. The Doctor sees value in the environment ("The Green Death," 1973), mindless slaves, like the Ood in "The Impossible Planet/The Satan Pit," mechanical robots, like K-9 ("The Invisible Enemy," 1977) and D84 ("The Robots of Death," 1977), and even destructive anti-universes ("It Takes You Away," 2018). These, and other examples, illustrate how the Doctor values all life, not just those who are rational.

A Life of Virtue

The life of virtue, sometimes called virtue or character ethics is one of our oldest moral traditions. First developed in Ancient Greece, it regained popularity over the past fifty years or so, mainly because of some of the problems noted with the two previous theories. The life of virtue is based on the ancient concept of *eudaimonism*. *Eudaimonism* is the Greek term for happiness, or well-being, and was used by ancient Greek philosophers, like Aristotle, the Stoics, and early Christian philosophers, but also, over the past several decades, has grown in popularity amongst contemporary ethicists like Alasdair MacIntyre.

According to Aristotle, all humans strive towards happiness, so a rational autonomous person would naturally do what best-ensures a life of happiness. For virtue ethicists, living a life of *virtue*—the active engagement of making good, moderate moral decisions—is the best way to ensure a person achieves happiness. We should, therefore, live a life engaged in the process of making good, virtuous decisions, which will hopefully produce a happy life out of the random events we're constantly confronted with.

A strong case can be made that the Doctor is a virtue ethicist, but there's a conceptual issue over the role of sympathy (feeling pain for) and compassion (feeling pain for *and* with) within virtue ethics that raises issues with its acceptance. Virtue ethics definitely requires sympathy, but it's unclear if it requires compassion; and compassion is a major feature of the Doctor's personality. Think of the Eleventh Doctor's final episode "The Time of the Doctor" (2013), where he gives up traveling and adventuring in order to spend the rest of his life protecting the people of Christmas from certain death. It wasn't necessary for him to stay, nor did he have any relationship to the people of Christmas or Trenzalore. Yet, his compassion led him to suffer with the people of Christmas, and even though it cost him many years and a leg in the process, he found a way to flourish. We'll return to this discussion in a few pages.

A Life of Care

The fourth conception of the good life is the life of care, which originates from feminist ethics, and is most commonly called "care ethics." Over the past several decades, it's become one of the most prominent ethical theories, and provides one of the most thoughtful and thorough criticisms of contemporary Western ethics. Care ethics is defined by its focus on promoting positive caring relationships, in light of the emotions and beliefs that result from our interpersonal relationships and our contextual needs in everyday life. Care ethics requires a relational understanding of reality where individuals exist in relation to each other, the inclusion of "outsiders," such as minorities, the mentally ill, and the physically disabled, and a consideration of issues from particular, contextual views. J.J. Silva, in *Doctor Who and Philosophy*, suggests the Doctor might in fact be a care ethicist, and many of the Doctor's actions support such an interpretation, but I would like to suggest something slightly different.

A Life of Needs

If the Doctor's ethics can be summed up in a brief statement, then a motto from existentialist, environmentalist, and outdoorsman Forrest Wood, Jr. comes the closest. Wood says, "I believe in 'getting in the thick of things'," which challenges us to act, make decisions, change the world around us, change ourselves, and learn first-hand how to answer life's most perplexing questions. For the Doctor, "getting in the thick of things" means that zie interferes with every person, society, species, and world—past, present, and future.

Nothing in the entire space-time continuum is safe from the Doctor's interference. Remember, that's why we called zir a flâneur.

In a set of recent books on justice, Nicholas Wolterstorff formulates an intriguing argument for an ethic of need, based on peace, which supports being a flâneur and "getting in the thick of things." The sort of peace that Wolterstorff discusses is not a state of tranquility where nothing bad happens, but instead, it's a state of peace where individuals are engaged in the world, learning about one's own and others' needs, while always striving to ensure all needs are met. In order for people's needs to be met, we all must work and challenge ourselves to not settle for tranquility but to strive for engagement. Being ethical, then, is about justice, a state of affairs where individuals get what they need. When individuals have their basic needs met, and help provide for the basic needs of others, a state of peace is created. This ethics of peace, unlike the virtue ethicist, calls on us to embrace the uncertainties of life and to accept our vulnerabilities. Once we accept the vulnerability of ourselves and others, we begin seeing the important role we all play in protecting one another, and so, we live our lives striving for peace.

The Doctor's awareness of others' pain is a continual theme in the New series. In "The Parting of the Ways" (2005), the Doctor claims he can hear "the sun and the moon, the day and the night . . . all there is, all there was, all there ever could be." He hears how they hurt, and it almost drives him mad. Other Time Lords don't appear to be afflicted with this suffering, yet the Doctor seems to embrace the pain and awareness that it creates. If the Doctor were trying to live the virtuous life or a life of pleasure, zie wouldn't continually subject himself to such torment. If the Doctor were simply concerned with following rational duties, zie wouldn't be concerned with inanimate objects like "the sun and the moon, day and night." What the Doctor illustrates over and over is a willingness to consider and seek out those who are in pain, and when zie finds them, he acts in ways to bring about a just state of affairs where such things can live in peace.

We've seen how complex and varied are the ways we can use the word 'good'. From the beauty of aesthetics to the right and wrong of ethics, 'good' is one of the most complex words in our human vocabulary. We could stop here, knowing we did some *good* work, but since we've opened the Pandorica of ethical goodness, let's move on to some major issues of right and wrong arising from *Doctor Who*.[1]

---

[1] An early version of this chapter first appeared in *Ruminations, Peregrinations, and Regenerations: A Critical Approach to Doctor Who* (Cambridge Scholars, 2010), edited by Christopher J. Hansen.

5
Monsters and Evil in *Doctor Who*

> There are some corners of the universe which have bred the most terrible things. Things which act against everything that we believe in. They must be fought.
>
> —SECOND DOCTOR, "The Moonbase," 1967

'Monster' is a word that gets thrown around a lot. We have legendary monsters like Dracula, Big Foot, and Loch Ness. We have what some people might call "pop culture monsters," like Kanye West, "Tot Mom," Nancy Grace, and (*insert your most-hated pop culture figure here*). Finally, of course, we have moral monsters like Adolf Hitler, Joseph Stalin, and Charles Manson. Are all of these "monsters?" If they are, then it's safe to assume that the term 'monster' is being used in different ways.

The first group are monsters because they are creatures, strangely alien and other-worldly. The second group are "monsters" because we don't like the way they act. We've vilified them to such a degree that they seem to be different than the rest of society's "normal" folk, so we call them monsters. The last group are monsters because they chose to participate and delight in the killing of innocent people, with no hint of regret or remorse.

We often do ourselves a disservice when we call our fellow humans 'monsters'. Doing so not only dehumanizes but also fictionalizes the person or thing we call 'monster'. Why might this be bad? Well, if we're to learn anything from these 'monsters', we need them to be like us. In other words, since we're human, we need them to be human. If we're not careful, calling a person a 'monster' can turn them into something non-human, something different, strange, and alien. They become something distant, an anomaly, something we don't have to worry about becoming because we're human, not monsters.

Take Hitler for instance: if he's turned into a non-human monster, then the Holocaust becomes a terrible fluke of history, one which we never have to worry about happening again; nor do we have to worry about "us" ever participating in the mass-extermination of innocents because we're "normal" humans that would never mass-exterminate innocents. As Jonathan Glover's *Humanity* disturbingly illustrates, such an intellectual position is false. Hitler was *all-too-human*, and just like all the people who helped Hitler achieve his goals, all of "us" good "normal" humans are just as *capable* of holding similar beliefs and acting in similar ways, whether we're willing to admit it or not.

Over the past fifty years *Doctor Who* has given us a plethora of monsters, ranging from the ludicrous—but quite tasty—Kandyman ("The Happiness Patrol," 1988) to the mundane, like human collaborators such as Luke Rattigan ("The Sontaran Stratagem" and "The Poison Sky," 2008). In between these extremes, viewers have faced Daleks, Cybermen, Zygons, Vashta Nerada, Weeping Angels, and among many others, Silents. Each one of *Doctor Who*'s monsters provides a fictional caricature of what it means for humans to be monsters. As Graham Sleight nicely illustrates in the book *The Doctor's Monsters*, each one exhibits a "narrowness" of behavior that is in tension with the Doctor's "flexibility." I think Sleight is correct in his analysis, and I would recommend his book for anyone truly interested in the nature of *Doctor Who*'s monsters, but I will take a different approach to examining the monsters of *Doctor Who*, since being a moral monsters has nothing to do with appearance.

Doctor Who typically associates being a monster with a person's evil motives and desires, so this is the approach taken below. So, to understand *Doctor Who*'s monsters, we need to understand evil, and to make sense of both, we'll examine some of *Doctor Who*'s most famous monsters.

What Makes a Monster?

To be a moral monster a person must carry out acts that we might call evil. 'Monster' implies a spectrum of wrongdoing. If all wrongdoing is monstrous, then the word 'monster' is meaningless, for it only means 'immoral', and if it only means 'immoral', then we're all monsters. There are certain Eastern and Western religious traditions that hold humans are naturally evil, which supports such a conclusion. Does the Doctor think humans are naturally evil?

As we've seen, the Doctor rejects the idea that humans are naturally evil. He even goes so far as to believe that Daleks are redeemable ("Into the Dalek,"

2014). The Doctor seems to agree with Laurence Thomas's conclusion that humans aren't naturally evil, though they can be easily motivated to both perform evil acts and allow evil acts to occur.

In *Vessels of Evil*, Thomas discusses American slavery and the Holocaust, and points to psychological studies like Philip Zimbardo's Stanford Prison Experiments and Stanley Milgram's experiments on the obedience to authority, to show how evil is perpetrated by ordinary fragile human beings. Our vulnerable fragility is often the root of our fears and feelings of inadequacy and hatred, and it's what makes us so susceptible to not only allowing evil to flourish but also to actively participate in evil. What often occurs is we strive to do what we feel to be right, but if we're not careful we can become morally sullied. Like an outfit that gets dirty and dingy over time, our moral character can become tainted; so much so that we can even find ourselves delighting in harmful acts. When we reach the point of delighting in harmful acts, we've become evil—what I refer to as a moral monster.

Based on this cursory understanding of what it means to be a moral monster, we can't say a thing is a monster simply by the way it looks. The Eleventh Doctor episode "Hide" (2013) provides us with a scary monster who not only haunts a mansion, but also haunts a different time zone. Viewers spend the entire episode fearing the "monster," which in the end, is nothing more than an alien creature trying to reunite with its long lost love. It might be part of humanity's common language to label the Crooked Man a "monster," but in terms of morality, it's a misuse of the word 'monster'. It's biased and offensive. It redefines 'monster' as 'ugly', and is no different than calling someone with a mental or physical defect a monster. If 'monster' is to have any moral weight, it must mean more than just 'ugly'. The concept of monster, then, must include some sort of evil or despicable behavior that is inconsistent with human morality.

There are fairly uncontroversial instances of evil—though as you might guess, when it comes to morality nothing is completely uncontroversial. Such evils include mass atrocities like genocide, rape camps, torture, and the indiscriminate killing of innocents. There are also more controversial instances of evil: violence in general, which includes war and capital punishment, manipulation, wickedness, and for some, anything that prevents a person's natural flourishing, which would include telling lies. To make things easy, and to get a glimpse of why there's disagreement over what is evil, let's make a helpful distinction between *quantitative* and *qualitative* evil. Quantitative evil maintains that an act like killing might be bad because it causes pain, or wrong because it violates a person's rights, but it isn't evil in itself. It only becomes evil when a certain quantity of people are killed. So, a Slitheen killing the Prime Minister of the United Kingdom is bad, but they didn't become evil until they started killing multiple people.

With quantitative evil, it's all about the numbers. One of the difficulties of quantitative evil is answering the question: "At what point does it become evil?" If we say a Dalek killing one human isn't evil, but a Dalek killing a thousand humans is evil; then, at what point did it become evil? Whatever number we choose appears random, since there appears to be no qualitative difference between any of the numbers. If 789 is the magic number, then what happens between it and 788 to make it evil? Nothing appears to have happened, except one more person has been murdered.

If there's no difference, then quantitative evil appears to be a hollow concept. So, instead of looking at the numbers, some see evil as a qualitative concept. Evil, then, is about the type of action performed, or the motives behind an action. The difference between 'murder' and 'kill' is a good illustration. By definition, murder is unjustified killing. In terms of the law, 'unjustified' means it breaks the law, but we're interested in morality, not legality. So, in terms of morality, 'unjustified' means there's no moral justification for such an act.

What's an example of justified killing? Self-defense is the most common example. If someone attacks you, and during your defense you inadvertently kill him, most ethicists (even many pacifists) will say your act is morally justified. It's this principle of self-defense that often grounds other arguments that involve killing: war, capital punishment, or abortion. When killing is unjustified, for whatever reason, it's considered murder, and if a person believes certain acts are evil, murder is one of the most obvious examples.

The proponent of qualitative evil maintains that something qualitatively different happens when a person commits certain acts. Using our Slitheen example from above, the Slitheen commit an evil act as soon as they murder another person. They didn't care that the Prime Minister was an autonomous person with a life and dreams. They only cared about themselves and their selfish desire to murder and sell the planet for profit. The Daleks, too, are evil because they go around enslaving and murdering people. In Trevor Baxendale's book *Prisoner of the Daleks*, the Daleks even calculate how to cause the most pain for the longest amount of time with their guns—evil indeed! So, not only do they murder, but they delight in the pain and suffering of creatures while they're dying. The Daleks' motives and delight in murdering are why they're so reviled by the Doctor as evil.

The distinction between quantitative and qualitative evil gives us a better understanding of what we should consider evil. Quantitative evil is an intuitively plausible concept, but it doesn't shed much light on why a person is evil. It's probably best just to admit that evil has a certain magnitude of wrongdoing, coupled with the intent of a wrongdoer, and avoid trying to pinpoint a specific number associated with when something becomes evil. Qualitative evil, and its ability to bring motivational desires into the discussion of immoral acts like murder, provides a stronger basis on which to make sense of evil and why some of *Doctor Who*'s villains are appropriately titled monsters.

A Silver Nemesis's Motives

One of my favorite "monsters" of *Doctor Who* is the Cybermen. In *Doctor Who and Philosophy: Bigger on the Inside*, I argue that the Cybermen aren't evil. Bonnie Green and Chris Willmott refer to my defense as the "altruistic interpretation" in their chapter "The Cybermen as Human.2," featured in *New Dimensions of Doctor Who*. I admit I tend to be overly sympathetic when it comes to the Cybermen, but if it's true that they have no emotions (leaving aside those annoying instances of writers giving them emotions for dramatic effect), then it seems impossible for them to be evil. I wholeheartedly agree that their willingness to harm and destroy creates extremely bad consequences, in the sense that it produces a lot of pain and suffering. However, they have no emotions, and so make no self-directed autonomous decisions or actions. As a result, they're more akin to a force of nature, which lacks any sort of intent or motive, than a monster.

It's true that Cybermen do a lot of really bad things, like persistently "upgrading" humans and killing anything and everything else that doesn't serve their purely logical interests. However, just because a thing performs bad actions, it doesn't necessarily mean that it's evil or it's done evil. The two moral theories of utilitarianism and duty ethics help us see how this is possible, because they make clear the difference between causing pain and doing wrong. Lots of things cause pain in life, but pain in itself isn't wrong. If it were, going to the dentist, going to school, and growing older, which all involve pain, would be wrong. For utilitarianism, what's important is that we perform actions or follow moral rules that create a balance of pleasure over pain, where pleasure is maximized as much as possible. So, for utilitarians, pain is bad, but it's not wrong.

For duty ethicists, pain has no moral standing. Morally motivated actions are either right or wrong. With duty ethics, then, we might have actions that are bad (they cause pain), but are morally right (they follow some moral principle); and we might have actions that are good (they cause pleasure), but are morally wrong (they violate a moral principle). With these distinctions the Cybermen should be understood as creating lots of bad, but due to their lack of autonomously generated motives, they shouldn't be understood as being evil. Crazy, right?! Not really. It's only crazy if you think natural disasters like hurricanes, volcanos, and tornados are evil. Let's examine motives more closely and see why natural disasters and Cybermen aren't evil.

A Cyber-Natural Disaster

Actions are based on our desires, and desires are what motivate action. One of the oldest theories of human action is "psychological egoism," which claims humans can only perform actions that are in their own self-interests. This theory is easy to verify. By performing an action, you've done what you wanted to do. Even if a Cyberman holds a gun to you and says, "Tell me where the Doctor is, or you will be deleted," it's your choice whether to talk or to remain silent. Your decision illustrates what you understand to be in your best interests.

If we assume psychological egoism is true, it still doesn't explain moral motives. Psychological egoism simply describes human psychology, and remember, ethics is concerned with how the world should be, not how the world is. Since humans have the freedom to choose how we act, even if we're driven by the motive to do what's in our own best interests, we can make complex moral decisions that conflict with our best interests. For instance, if you remain silent when the Cyberman asks you the location of the Doctor, then you're putting the life of the Doctor and his interests over your own life. As a result, even though you're choosing to do what you want to do, which supports psychological egoism, your value system motivates you to do what's best for the Doctor—and whoever else zie happens to be saving at the time.

This other-centered approach is called altruism. Altruists consider the desires and needs of others and act in such a way to make sure their needs are met; indeed, sometimes at the expense of one's own desires and needs. I've already argued that the Doctor operates on a similar moral principle, but counter to my argument in *Doctor Who and Philosophy*, it's impossible for the Cybermen to be altruists, or any other sort of egoist. In fact, if what we know about the Cybermen is true, that they lack any sort of emotions, then they can't make any sort of volitional acts independent of their "programming." Except for maybe the Cyber Controller/ Leader, most Cybermen act as mere automatons, so they seem no different than a poorly programmed computer. If they had desires, and the emotional states that ground desires, then we could fault them for not trying to be better, or to correct their programming flaws. Since they lack such desires and emotions, then it'd be wrong to call them evil.

Evil requires volition, and one of the best accounts of volition comes from David Hume. In *A Treatise of Human Nature*, Hume argues that human action isn't motivated by reason alone—a pretty radical idea at the time. Since at least the time of Socrates, reason was thought to be the mechanism behind human action. Hume argues, instead, that intentional actions come from passions. These passions are most often simply the result of instinctual responses to stimuli like pleasure and pain. A cool wind causes me to want a jacket, or the empty feeling in my stomach makes me long for something tasty to eat. A stimulus creates a passion, which creates a desire, which then motivates us to satisfy the desire. Reason plays no role in the creation of desires and motives. For Hume, reason only arises when we set out to satisfy our desires, by helping us reason how best to go about satisfying it.

Without the desire for a jacket or food, we wouldn't seek such things. If we had no desires, then we'd never seek out anything. So, if all we have is logic and reason, and no emotional passions, then we'd never have desires or the motive to seek out anything. We'd be mindless automatons, following some pre-programmed motive, and as a result, we wouldn't be morally autonomous. We'd be more like a force of nature that has no intentions, motives, desires, or any other sort of moral component. Hume's argument is the true weakness of Cybermen, because it shows that if Cybermen are truly motivated by pure logic, free from pain, fear, and for the most part, death ("The Tenth Planet," 1966), then they aren't moral beings. They're simply poorly-programmed machines, and no matter how annoying and dangerous a poorly-programmed machine is, it's wrong to call such a thing evil. If they aren't evil, or even capable of being moral, then they aren't moral monsters.

In the New series, where Cybermen are created by John Lumic to rid humans of pain and suffering, they lack all human emotions, which means they lack all desires ("The Rise of the Cybermen"/"Age of Steel," 2006). Instead of human emotions responding to stimuli, they are programmed to respond to stimuli. This difference means Cybermen don't voluntarily choose to perform an action; instead, their programming determines what they choose. It's like the difference between you saying: "I chose to watch *Doctor Who*" and "My DVR chose to record *Doctor Who*." The former required volition, while the latter simply followed a programmed command.

We can criticize John Lumic and the logicians from the Classic series for how they programmed the Cybermen, and we can call them moral monsters, but it's a misuse of the term to call Cybermen monsters. They're more like a natural disaster, and though there are some who refer to hurricanes and tornadoes as "natural evils," I would argue—and I think the Doctor would agree—that calling such things "evil" is wrong, especially since we always find the Doctor fighting against the monster causing the natural disaster, not the disaster itself ("Enemy of the World," 1968 and "The Fires of Pompeii," 2008)—unless zie knows of a way of preventing it. Even then, zie's fighting to save people's lives, not fighting against the disaster.

Dalek Hatred

The Daleks and Cybermen share many similarities, but they're markedly different. No, not because it only takes three Daleks to wipe out a Cyberarmy, but because the Daleks have emotions. Granted, they only have a set of limited emotions, and depending on the needs of a particular story, they're sometimes portrayed as being as mindless and logical as Cybermen. The majority of Dalek lore, however, shows that they are driven by the emotions of hatred and superiority. No matter how limited, these are emotions, and so it's appropriate to call Daleks both evil and monstrous.

Hatred in itself isn't evil. I hate seeing young children starved, mistreated, and abused. When I see such things, my hatred of them motivates me to stand up and act, to help those in need. This is exactly what the Doctor does in "The Beast Below" (2010), when he reveals he can't stand off to the side and do nothing when he hears a child cry. So, what makes hatred evil?

The answer isn't easy. Hatred typically clouds the mind and prevents clear rational thought. It makes us do rash things, like summarily judging and killing evil despots like Solomon ("Dinosaurs on a Spaceship," 2012), which is contrary to the "way we roll" ("A Town Called Mercy," 2012).

Hatred can also focus the mind, so much so that our vision becomes myopic—we focus on one thing while ignoring everything around us. When our vision becomes myopic, we often become willfully blind to the harms and wrongdoings we commit. We see this happen when species like the Zygons, Silurians, and the Saturnyns from "Vampires of Venice" (2010) are driven to destroy other species by the hatred of their possible extinction. Their hatred, then, causes them to not only destroy innocent lives and the moral principles of justice that might ground their society, but to cause their own destruction in the process.

The Daleks, however, exhibit a different sort of hatred. Their hatred, often considered analogous of Nazism, is a hatred of all things impure and different from themselves. Jonathan Glover examines the moral history of the twentieth century in *Humanity*, and he attributes much of the evil of the century to "tribalism" and closed "belief systems." Tribalism manifests itself in a "us vs. them" mentality, which turns "them"—the Other—into something dangerous—a disease, a cancer, and mortal threat. Closed belief systems, sometimes simply referred to as ideologies, are marked by a controlled set of beliefs that cares little for truth and allows no dissension. Closed belief systems are the hallmark of fundamentalist political and religious groups who reject facts and reason and are willing to harm and kill those who disagree, like the fundamentalist racist regimes of the Nazis and the Ku Klux Klan, and the ideological regimes of Communist Russia and Maoist China.

The Daleks' evil and monstrousness is grounded in tribalism and a closed belief system. Their tribe is the Daleks, and if anyone is even slightly different, they are both inferior and unworthy of shared existence. Even fellow "Daleks" run the risk of becoming too different, as seen in "Evolution of the Daleks" (2007), "Victory of the Daleks" (2010), and the oft-referred to Dalek civil war ("Remembrance of the Daleks," 1988). Davros isn't even immune from the hatred of the Daleks ("Genesis of the Daleks," 1975 and "Resurrection of the Daleks," 1984). Their tribalism reinforces their belief system of hatred and domination that sees the universe as belonging to the Daleks, to be used as they see fit.

Dalek tribalism and their belief system is only possible if they have some sort of emotion that motivates action. Even though they lack emotions like compassion and concepts like friendship, they're capable of transcending their natural tendencies. Humans share many Dalek tendencies and motives, but most of us choose not to act upon them in our daily lives. Granted, for dramatic effect, the writers often present the Daleks as lacking a "human perspective" ("The Evil of the Daleks," 1967 and "Evolution of the Daleks"), but from the history of the Daleks we don't see on TV, the Daleks continuously make complex decisions about how to live their lives and structure society. We could say it's in their nature and so they can't do anything about it. If we take this approach, then there's no morality—the worst possible conclusion, since all natural desires (killing, raping, abusing, for instance) would be morally acceptable. We should, instead, understand the Daleks as being capable of growing and learning from their complex emotional desires, no matter how limited they are in relation to humans. Like humans, they might choose not to overcome their base-desires, but that makes them even more responsible for their wrongdoing.

For audiences, then, the lesson to be learned is that when we dogmatically believe in a closed belief system, and we see our "tribe"—whether it's our community, country, religion, or species—as the only valuable one, we exhibit Dalek tendencies of being evil moral monsters. We should instead strive to overcome our natural desires to do wrong, and to stand by while wrongdoing occurs, and instead strive to live morally engaged lives.

The Evil of Manipulation

Being a monster doesn't require you to go around killing a bunch of innocent people. In fact, our typical human monsters never kill anyone. Did Hitler ever actually kill anyone? Yes, he ordered and is responsible for the death of millions, but did he ever personally take anyone's life? Bernie Madoff destroyed people's lives, and some of these people committed suicide, but he never murdered anyone. Parents around the globe abuse their children, both physically and mentally. Some even sell their children into prostitution and slavery. Spouses manipulate and abuse each other, and among many other instances of evil, some corporations knowingly enslave, poison, and kill innocent people, usually the ones making and using their products. Where is this sort of evil in *Doctor Who*?

Like real life, these sorts of evil are simply woven into the fabric of the show. We see it occur when the Ood are enslaved ("Planet of the Ood," 2008). The Nestene Consciousness often materializes as part of a broader corporation ("Spearhead from Space," 1970). Children are often harmed and manipulated (Arguably, all of Amy Pond's episodes are the result of her being manipulated, 2010–2012).

I could spend a book just talking about these "everyday" evils. Instead, let's focus on one particular type of evil that is arguably one of the most common human evils: manipulation. Of course, if we're going to talk about manipulation, then there's no greater example of manipulation than the Master/Missy. From his devious machinations with the Axons ("The Claws of Axos," 1971) to her attempt to make the Doctor the "President" of the universe ("Dark Water/Death in Heaven," 2014), and even his killing and masquerading as O in "Spyfall" (2020), the Master presents us with a very human monster—a person who lies and deceives to get everything zie wants.

You might be saying, "You're kidding, right. I'm nothing like the Master/Missy." Think about every time you've wanted something, and in order to get it, you've told a lie. I couldn't turn in my paper because my grandmother died. I was speeding because I had to get some place really important, or simply, I wasn't speeding. I don't feel good and can't come into work today. I don't have any change. I think you look great. I don't know how that got there!

Why is it so easy and natural to lie? As we see on "The Time of the Doctor" (2013), even the Doctor struggles with telling the truth. The good news is that just because you lie, it doesn't mean you're a monster. Telling lies, however, can morph you into a monster, because lying is a form of disrespect and manipulation. It helps us get what we want without facing the possible dangers of telling the truth. The Master, then, gives us a nice illustration of the type of monster we resemble when we make lying and manipulation habit.

Most of us won't go around trying to conquer the world with our lies, but lying and manipulation is an attempt to conquer our own little world. If we go around trying to conquer through lying and manipulation, we'll become our own version of the Master/Missy. However, if we go around conquering the world through compassion and understanding, we'll become our own version of the Doctor. As Friedrich Nietzsche suggests in *The Will to Power*, much of life involves trying to shape the world according to our will. It's up to us to choose how we go about shaping the world. You can shape it by being evil and manipulative, or by being persistent and compassionate. Regardless of how you engage the world, it's up to you to decide whether your passions are moral, and whether or not you're going to act upon them. Of course, there are exceptions to the rule, for some cognitive disorders prevent fully-volitional acts. In such cases we should help, or provide the help needed that will allow such individuals to flourish in their own way.

We're greater than Cybermen because we have the will to choose how to act. Sometimes we resemble Daleks with our close-minded tribalism, but no matter how limited our emotional states, we can always rise above our natural tendencies—at least that's what the Doctor teaches. Just like Daleks, we can sometimes resemble many of the moral monsters on *Doctor Who*, which provide us with a reflection of ourselves; and if we pay attention, we can learn how to change ourselves from being monsters to being heroes.

The Wrath of the Doctor

That is the role you seem determined to play, so it seems that I must play mine! The man that stops the monsters!

—TWELFTH DOCTOR, "Flatline," 2014

We've already looked at many instances of how the Doctor responds to the challenges of life, and I've argued that one of the key features of the Doctor's understanding of the good life is that we must recognize our own vulnerability. By recognizing these vulnerabilities, and the power we have over whether we help or harm others, we begin to see ourselves as part of an inter-connected moral community with all other moral entities. So, instead of being afraid and hiding our vulnerabilities, we should embrace them and engage the world, with full knowledge that we might get hurt in the process, attempting to make the world and ourselves a little better in the process.

Sadly, however, there's evil in the world, and the more we engage, the more we're likely to be harmed and wronged. It's simply a fact of life that by accident, or by careful planning, people wrong each other, and yes, we wrong other people. So, how should we respond to wrongdoing? The justice of punishment, called retributive justice (think retribution), is complex and diffi-cult. How do we determine what a wrongdoer deserves? Is it enough to say, "An eye for an eye?" Is this a limit on what we can do, meaning *no more* than an eye may be taken? Or is it a prescription, saying we must take an eye? If it's the latter, then how do we determine equal punishment? If someone murders your friend, then is the "equal" punishment to murder their friend? That can't be right.

Philosophers of law will often talk about the arbitrar-iness of laws and punishments. Basically, legislators create a list of crimes ranked in order from bad to worst; then after creating a similar list of punishments, they try to match both up. Since there are no laws found in nature that tell us how we should punish, like all mur-derers should be killed, we must rely on ethics to justify what should happen. Even when we let reason rule over our emotions and passions, determining appropriate moral punishments can seem as arbitrary as determin-ing legal punishments. So, what sort of approach does the Doctor take to punishment?

The Doctor Dances

It's often said, it takes two to tango. Well, except in in-stances of self-wronging, it also takes at least two to be wronged. You need a perpetrator who wrongs another person, and you need a victim who is the recipient of the wrongdoing. When a wrongdoing occurs both per-petrator and victim deserve something. Morally speak-ing, the perpetrator deserves blame or punishment, while the victim deserves some sort of restitution. In everyday language, we usually say they both deserve justice, and perpetrators and victims both "get justice" when perpetrators are properly punished. When perpetrators aren't properly punished, an injustice occurs.

This sort of language is often too simplistic and obscures the true nature of retributive justice. First off, no one "gets" justice. Justice isn't *the punishment* a wrongdoer gets, nor is it the money a victim receives. It might require such things, but it isn't an object to be given. Justice is a state of affairs, a moral relationship between people, one that prescribes certain actions be performed after a wrongdoing.

Second, moral and legal justice are two different things, yet we must not ignore that within civil society they're intimately intertwined. If my wife dies as a result of Ms. Gillyflower's despicable plan in "The Crimson Horror" (2013), she's violated my wife's moral and legal rights not to be murdered. As a result of the violation of her legal right, the police should arrest and the courts should punish Ms. Gillyflower. They don't arrest and prosecute her for violating my wife's moral right. If Ms. Gillyflower promised my wife to introduce her to Mr. Sweet, but never did, then she's violated my wife's moral right not to be lied to; but the police aren't going to come arrest her for such a lie. Civil society is in charge of punishment relating to legal rights, and individuals are in charge of moral punishments. In civil society, the legal and the moral will often overlap, but not always. Let's look at some possible difficulties.

If Ms. Gillyflower slapped my wife, then an appropriate moral punishment might be that my wife gets to slap her back. But if she murders my wife, then my wife has no way of punishing her. The burden falls to my wife's loved ones, like me. I, then, have several options. I can scorn, resent, and among other things, hate Ms. Gillyflower, but in a civil society I'm supposed to let the law determine her punishment and hope that it prevails in quenching my moral outrage. When the legal system works, we call this both legal and moral justice.

As we all know, however, the law doesn't always work. Crooked judges and lawyers, news media, social pressures, ignorance, jury tampering, and among a whole host of other things, common human error can all prevent justice from occurring. Peter French provides an excellent examination of when justice fails in *Cowboy Metaphysics* and *The Virtues of Vengeance*. Especially in the latter, French argues that vengeance is tied to our basic moral intuitions about justice and punishment. When society's laws adequately punish wrongdoers, then our motive for vengeance is quenched, but when a legal system fails to properly punish wrongdoers, vengeance motivates us to achieve justice by other means. In other words, when legal justice fails, according to French, we're morally justified in seeking appropriate means of vengeful punishment.

French's argument is nuanced and complex, and he doesn't promote vengeance *carte blanche*. Instead, vengeance is seen as the careful consideration of carrying out the appropriate punishment for the wrong committed. In other words, we must treat like cases alike. So, if Ms. Gillyflower wrongs me by murdering my wife, and the legal system fails to prosecute her—and, of course, the Doctor and Paternoster Gang isn't there to help—I have the *moral* right to exact my revenge, even if it means I wind up in jail for violating legal codes. This is where things get difficult.

She murdered my wife, so the punishment should be something similar. Yet, there appears to be no corollary punishment. First, Ms. Gillyflower didn't murder me, so me killing her isn't the same. In fact, since I have to suffer the pain of having my loved one unjustly taken away from me, killing Ms. Gillyflower might be letting her off too easy. Ms. Gillyflower robbed me of the person I love, so the like thing to do would be to murder someone she loves.

The problem with this punishment is: if I murder an innocent person, then I become a murderer, and deserve to be punished for murdering an innocent person. We might say, from my wife's perspective, Ms. Gillyflower murdered her, so my killing of Ms. Gillyflower is simply me claiming the rights of my deceased wife. In such a case, I would serve as a representative of my wife, taking care of business she was unable to complete due to Ms. Gillyflower's actions. The problem with this approach is that my wife was innocent and didn't deserve death, but Ms. Gillyflower isn't innocent. Unlike my wife, she's guilty and deserves punishment. So, the killing of Ms. Gillyflower doesn't carry with it the same moral weight. Is this close enough for justice? I don't know, but I hope you're starting to see how difficult it is to "properly" punish someone, and not just randomly pick a punishment.

Once we allow for moral vengeance, we open ourselves to these sorts of difficult issues, which usually lead to blood-feuds. Legal codes serve as the foundation of civil society and are designed to avoid such issues and feuds. From the law of the Israelites found in the Hebrew scriptures to the Roman legal codes, which inspired the Germanic legal codes and eventually all of

Europe and America, legal codes provide a means of escape from the cycle of violence that often erupts as a result of individuals seeking their own moral justice through vengeance.

One way to approach resolving some of these issues is to figure out the purpose of retributive justice. Is justice achieved when the proper punishment is carried out, or is it achieved when the wrongdoer is rehabilitated, or is it when wrongdoers and victims achieve reconciliation?

Which Way to the Just?

A person's sense of retributive justice often depends on the "direction" in which they think justice occurs. For many, justice is backward-looking. There are a set of rules, and when one is violated, we "look back" to see exactly what happened, and dole out the appropriate punishment prescribed for such an offense. Opposed to a backward-looking approach is a forward-looking approach, which looks at the violation and determines the type of punishment that will produce the best outcome.

The implications of these two approaches are vast. If you're backward-looking, then all you're interested in is the act and the prescribed punishment. Any consideration of outcomes is outside of the scope of justice. If you're forward-looking, then punishment is at best an attempt to make amends and possibly rehabilitate the perpetrator.

There are shortcomings to each approach, and instead of picking one or the other, the Doctor suggests we should develop a way of thinking about retributive justice that involves looking backwards, forwards, and "in between." In fact, the Doctor's approach shifts focus away from retributive justice (punishment), and suggests that we should primarily care about providing for people's needs. The Doctor's "in between" is based on his ethic of needs, which requires us to always take into account what each party needs, both wrongdoers and victims, and determine what will bring about better people and a better world. The Doctor's approach helps us avoid the implications of Isaac Asimov's mantra in *Foundation*: "Never let your sense of morals get in the way of doing what is right," for when we get so caught up in our desire for our own particular ideas of "proper" punishment, we tend to perform all sorts of unjust deeds. If we instead focus on what people need, and we train ourselves to act justly, then what we consider punishment will be transformed into something much different than we're used to in contemporary society.

Think about what might go wrong if you only take a backward-looking approach. You lose the ability to take into account any extenuating circumstances, which might tell you that the wrongdoer deserves less (or more) than the prescribed punishment. For instance, the Doctor's first on-screen action involves him abducting two school teachers ("An Unearthly Child," 1963). If you're only interested in what laws were broken, then you should respond like a good Judoon: hunt him down, and swiftly execute the proper punishment. Such an approach might work in some instances but, as in the Doctor's case, it's too harsh. It ignores all sorts of important moral features. Proper punishment requires a consideration of all the facts, motives, and extenuating circumstances, which is why a backward-looking approach by itself won't do, and why the Doctor criticizes the Judoon's type of justice.

Similar problems arise if we only take a forward-looking approach. The moral theory of utilitarianism, which tells us to maximize pleasure and minimize pain for all involved, serves as a good example of a forward-looking approach. One of the most prominent arguments against utilitarianism is that it allows for injustice. As John Rawls discusses in "Two Concepts of Rules," future consequences are the only morally relevant features a utilitarian should consider when determining punishment. Because of this, utilitarians don't care about the past. They only care about what'll bring about the most good over bad, all things considered. The downside of this moral position is that it provides a conceptual basis for punishing *innocent* people, if doing so brings about enough overall good. Such injustices will be rare, since punishing innocent people will typically bring about more pain than pleasure, especially for the innocent person who is punished. Still, this is a deeply troubling conceptual flaw.

When the Doctor abducts Ian and Barbara, what does he deserve? We might say that putting up with Ian and Barbara's hard-headedness is punishment enough, but their stubbornness was probably justified. In terms of a backward-looking approach, we would punish the Doctor for abducting Ian and Barbara, and we might punish them for forced entry into the TARDIS. In terms of a forward-looking approach, we would have to determine what punishment would bring about the most good. It's tempting just to say, the Doctor does so much good, we should let him go free, but you could also argue that a lot of the good he does is only needed because of his interfering. For instance, it's the Doctor who stirs up the Dalek "hornets' nest" in both "The

Daleks" (1963) and "Genesis of the Daleks" (1975). In the Doctor's case, then, a forward-looking approach provides little guidance.

Now, if we add a needs-based analysis of the situation, we can take into account the above, and we can also look at how Ian and Barbara's travels with the Doctor enriched their lives. We can list all of the people they saved on their journeys. We can also consider how their travels influenced the Doctor to become kinder and gentler—the most popular example being when Ian prevents the Doctor from murdering the caveman in "An Unearthly Child."

By focusing on needs, we're allowed to examine all of the relevant features of the case (backwards, forwards, sideways) and determine that not only were Ian and Barbara not wronged by being abducted, but all things considered, everyone is better off as a result of their nosiness and the Doctor's paranoia. Like good flâneurs, Ian, Barbara, and the Doctor were all living engaged lives, following their instincts to help a young girl. They were all trying to provide for the needs of others. As a result, they ended up joining forces, traveling together, helping others, and saving planets. They all got what they needed. We only arrive at this conclusion if we're willing to look at the case not only from a punishment point of view, but also a needs-based point of view. By carefully examining the case, we discover no wrong has occurred; so no punishment is deserved.

Let's make things a little more difficult. What sort of punishment does the Doctor deserve from the Time Lords for stealing an old Type-40 TARDIS, violating the Time Lord policy of non-interference, and breaking the rules of time? These are serious crimes, akin to treason, and the Time Lords continually struggle with what the Doctor deserves. The Doctor has broken the law, yet zie does so many good things, sometimes at the request of the Time Lords. In "The War Games" (1969), they exile him and force a regeneration. During the Tom Baker years (1974–1981) he's continually badgered to work for them, and even courted as Time Lord president— punishment indeed! In "The Trial of a Time Lord" (1986), he's put on trial for his meddling, by the New series he's portrayed as a nuisance—a gadfly, best ignored ("The Day of the Doctor," 2013), and Capaldi's Doctor becomes a rogue again by breaking all sorts of Time Lord laws (Season Nine).

Even though the Doctor has violated Time Lord law, because the Doctor is dedicated to doing good, and he actually achieves the good, the idea of punishment doesn't apply. To say the Doctor deserves punishment for doing what is just, is a misuse of language, and it's why the Time Lords struggle with how to punish him. Their backward-looking rules say one thing, their forward-looking intuitions tell them another, and in between you have the Doctor doing what's necessary to help others and to protect the universe from evil.

What have we decided, so far? First, we need to be clear about how we understand the purpose of punishment. Second, we've seen that *Doctor Who* suggests we approach justice by focusing on doing good and providing for other's needs, and when issues of retributive justice arise, we use the same approach to determine what sort of wrong has been committed and what's actually deserved.

Regular viewers of *Doctor Who* know this is only half of the story, for the Doctor also challenges us to have mercy and to forgive, both of which give wrongdoers less than they deserve. If this is true, then are mercy and forgiveness unjust?

Justice Without Punishment?

As already noted, retributive justice requires a punishment that matches the wrong committed. Yet, the Doctor's needs-based ethic often tells us to give wrongdoers less than they deserve by having compassion, showing mercy, and granting forgiveness. So, can we have justice without proper punishment? The Doctor would say, "Yes." Let's see why, and I'll let you decide if zie is right.

In terms of morality, the most common punishment for victims is that of holding resentment (moral anger) towards the wrongdoer. Punishment is supposed to quench our resentment. Of course, there might be times when someone wrongs us and we don't feel resentment. A child might call the Ninth Doctor "big ears," and because it's a child, the Doctor might just ignore her; but he might resent an adult, like Mikey Smith, who did the same—he might even respond by calling him Rickey! Instead of feeling resentment and seeking punishment, we might respond by doing something like granting forgiveness and reducing the wrongdoer's punishment. Yet, if wrongdoers deserve resentment, and forgiveness forswears resentment, then forgiveness is unjust, because the wrongdoer doesn't get what he deserves.

The Doctor's needs-based ethic asks us to look *back* at the wrong committed, then look *forward* to what will bring about the best consequences. In between these two considerations, we must also examine the needs of the wrongdoer, in order to determine the character and needs of the person. The Doctor's approach recognizes that a wrong has been committed and that it deserves punishment. It then examines the needs of the wrongdoer (and victim) to determine what other moral features must be taken into consideration. Finally, it takes all of the information and arrives at a punishment that takes into account all morally relevant information and suggests a punishment that's not only best for, but also what's needed by, all parties involved.

Think of Commander Lytton, who appeared in two episodes: "Resurrection of the Daleks" (1984) and "Attack of the Cybermen" (1985). In the former episode, he aided the Daleks in their rescue of Davros. In the latter episode, he appears to aid the Cybermen in their plot to crash Halley's Comet into Earth, thereby, preventing the destruction of Mondas in "The Tenth Planet" (1966). Throughout both stories, Lytton is portrayed as the evil collaborator, only concerned with his own gain. He fights with the Doctor, and the Doctor does his best to thwart his plans. However, by the end of "Attack of the Cybermen" we find out that Lytton is helping the Cryons fight against the Cybermen. After discovering his mistake, the Doctor realizes he's "never misjudged anyone quite so badly . . ."

Lytton provides a nice example of how we don't always know the motives behind people's actions. In fact, with Lytton it's unclear how much of Lytton still exists after the Dalek "conditioning" of "Resurrection of the Daleks." What's clear is that the Doctor is anguished over his resentment and desire to punish Lytton. Even though Lytton committed several immoral acts, the Doctor's awareness of the *entire* situation suggests that if Lytton had survived, the Doctor would've forgiven his actions and let him go without any sort of punishment. He does the same for Sabalom Glitz ("The Trial of a Time Lord" and "Dragonfire," 1987), and arguably, Rusty in "Into the Dalek" (2014). The Doctor sees something within these immoral agents, and instead of giving them the punishment they deserve, zie does something different. Zie tries to reform and help them reach their full potential. As we see with Rusty, it doesn't always work, but that's part of the process. The Doctor's ethic of need doesn't require us to be successful, but it does challenge us to try.

The key is to show how the Doctor's account of distributive justice—his ethic of need—is consistent with retributive justice; that giving wrongdoers less than they deserve is just. In his book *Justice in Love*, Nicholas Wolterstorff provides a useful distinction between pure retributive punishment and what he refers to as "reprobative punishment." Where retribution is considered backward-looking, reprobative punishment attempts to do what we see the Doctor do: "to condemn what was done and to send a message of non-condonation." Reprobative punishment, then, is a type of punishment that is concerned with the welfare of the wrongdoer—it accepts the repentance of the wrongdoer, and seeks a lesser punishment designed to respect both the wrongdoer and the victim. So, when someone commits a wrongful act, the Doctor doesn't just condemn them to such-and-such punishment. Instead, zie investigates their motives and knowledge, while trying to understand and reform them, in order for them to receive what they deserve and (if possible) flourish.

Think of all of the examples of evil we mentioned above. In each case, the Doctor investigates, learns, and offers them a way out. From "vampires" in Venice ("Vampires in Venice," 2010) and gaseous aliens in Cardiff ("The Unquiet Dead," 2005), to two-dimensional creatures in Bristol ("Flatline"), the Doctor offers help, and in order to help, zie must know what these aliens need. The Doctor doesn't condone the wrongful actions of invaders, but as we see in "Flatline," he recognizes they may not understand the extent to which they are wronging other moral beings. So, zie sets zirs energies towards finding a way of stopping the invaders, one that respects their moral worth. Even when the Doctor finds invaders to be evil, zie most-often offers them an escape. When they fail to take the escape, the Doctor stops them because zie's the Doctor and the one who stops the monsters.

The Doctor's Journey to Forgiveness

Before stopping, we have one more path to journey down, and it's the path of forgiveness, especially of self-forgiveness. Forgiveness is one of humanity's most complex moral concepts. On the one hand, it's deeply personal. Each one of us has an idea of what forgiveness is and when and how we should forgive. On the other hand, forgiveness is fundamentally relational. It involves other people, even if the "other person" is yourself. So, no matter how personal forgiveness is, it's always a relational concept.

As we've seen, forgiveness is sometimes at odds with justice, since forgiveness tells us to give wrongdoers less than they deserve. Reprobative justice helps to some degree, by illustrating that wrongdoers sometimes deserve mercy and forgiveness. Forgiveness, however, can at times be so extreme that it offers no punishment at all, or a punishment so different that it doesn't seem to fit the deed. Let's look at some of the issues, especially those relating to the Doctor's inner-turmoil and attempt to forgive himself.

For the most part, Classic *Doctor Who* doesn't have a lot to say about forgiveness, but by the time you get to the New series, forgiveness and its related concepts take center stage. The Doctor now apologizes to enemies, seeks the redemption of friends and enemies alike, and maybe most importantly, longs to be rid of the torment and guilt of zirs actions during the last Great Time War. Zie wants the peace and reconciliation that forgiveness promises.

The Time War, along with the Fiftieth Anniversary Special "The Day of the Doctor," allows us to frame the Doctor's life as one long journey. Resembling the Christian parable of the prodigal son, his journey hasn't been easy, nor does he always make the right decisions; but in the end, zie comes to terms with zirself, is accepted by zirs people, and is even granted a new set of regenerations. True, the Doctor creates some new enemies in "Hell Bent" (2015), and the fate of the Time Lords is unclear by the time we reach "The Timeless Children"; but I'm sure they'll find a way to co-exist in the future.

Nevertheless, the Doctor's journey hasn't been easy, and I'd like to examine two particular episodes, which I take to be parables of the Doctor's self-punishment and zirs journey towards self-forgiveness. The first episode is "Dinosaurs on a Spaceship" (2012). In this episode, the Doctor encounters Solomon, a space "trader"—in other words, pirate—who not only hijacked a Silurian spaceship but also ejected them into space. Solomon didn't kill the Silurians because of some deeply held ideological belief or because he thought they were evil. No, he killed them because they stood in the way of something he wanted: profit. Solomon knew what he was doing, and he knew it was wrong. Yet, he did it anyway, and even delighted in doing it. If that wasn't enough, he shoots the triceratops right in front of the Doctor with the same calm, disinterested greed. So, when it came time for Solomon to be punished, the Doctor showed no hesitation punishing him with death.

It isn't shocking to see Solomon executed—your intuitions probably tell you he deserves it. What's shocking is that the Eleventh Doctor condemns Solomon to death so easily. Something has changed, which is exactly what Amy Pond points out in the next episode "A Town Called Mercy" (2012):

> THE DOCTOR: We could end this right now. We could save everyone right now!
>
> AMY: This is not how we roll, and you know it. What's happened to you, Doctor? When did killing someone become an option?
>
> THE DOCTOR: Jex has to answer for his crimes.
>
> AMY: And what then? Are you going to hunt down everyone who's made a gun or a bullet or a bomb?
>
> THE DOCTOR: But they keep coming back, don't you see? Every time I negotiate, I try to understand. Well not today. No, today I honor the victims first. His, the Master's, the Daleks'. All the people that died because of my mercy!
>
> AMY: See this is what happens when you travel alone for too long. Well listen to me, Doctor, we can't be like him. We have to be better than him.

Notice how pained the Doctor is by his "mercy." He's seen the result of his mercy, and he's tired of seeing it lead to the deaths of innocent people. This is such a powerful moment because it illustrates not only the Doctor's vulnerability, but also the difficulties of reprobative punishment. During his time of weakness, he's come to the conclusion that it's easier just to kill off villains, and he's right: it is easier. There's no questioning or thinking. It's kill quickly and move on, just like we saw in "Dinosaurs on a Spaceship." Amy points out the flaw in his logic: once you say, "Execute those who cause killing," then we must start executing all killers. We start with the killers, move to the makers of weapons, and end with the people who pay taxes, which support the manufacturers and governments involved in killing. This line of reasoning might be good for some, but it isn't for the Doctor. It's not how he rolls.

In "A Town Called Mercy," Kahler-Jex serves as a mirror of the Doctor. Jex killed many innocent people in order to create a weapon that would bring about peace, by killing millions of enemies. When Jex stands up to the Doctor, defiantly defending his war crimes, the Doctor hears his own attempt to justify the killing of millions to achieve peace, and he sees its hollowness. Just as the Doctor would like to eradicate "the Doctor" who committed those crimes, he sets out to eradicate *doctor* Jex.

One clever conceptual twist in the episode is that Kahler-Tek, the Gunslinger, also mirrors the Doctor. Tek wants revenge on the person who ruined his life and caused him to kill millions, and he's willing to "tear the universe apart" in order to achieve his own peace. These two characters illustrate the struggle that goes on within the Doctor's psyche. As made clear in "The Day of the Doctor," the Doctor is at war with himself. He's yet to be punished for his deeds during the Time War, and his internal battle manifests itself in "A Town Called Mercy."

Forgiveness doesn't occur in "A Town Called Mercy," but the first step towards forgiveness happens, and it's mercy. Jex breaks the cycle of violence and hatred by recognizing Tek, and by ending his own life, in order to save Tek from having one more death on his conscience. Freed from the torment of revenge, Tek is able to not only find his own personal peace, but he also becomes an agent of peace, protecting the people of Mercy. This is what the Doctor needs.

After the execution of Solomon, the Doctor too is able to take the first step towards forgiveness. With Amy's reminder and Jex's and Tek's examples, the Doctor finds himself one step closer to coming to terms with his actions during the Time War. It's with all of this inner-turmoil in mind that the Eleventh Doctor's refusal to use the Moment in "The Day of the Doctor" becomes his moment of peace. It's the peace of resolving his inner-turmoil that gives him the opportunity to recognize himself in the War Doctor. He's able to wipe the slate clean by "killing" the War Doctor, through the act of recognizing him as the man who was the Doctor on the day it was impossible to be the Doctor. It's this step towards self-forgiveness that reinvigorates his life of protecting the universe. So, if we understand the Doctor's fictional tale of avoiding the mass extermination of the Time Lords as a parable for how we must find ways to work through our own inner-turmoil, maybe one day we too can forgive, stop punishing ourselves, and begin to flourish.

I'm Going Home

I will end this chapter with a story of punishment from Arun Gandhi (Mahatma Gandhi's grandson). In a short piece entitled "A Recollection," Arun reminisces about taking his father to an all-day conference. While at the conference, he was supposed to get the car serviced. As many kids would do, he played around, saw a movie, and showed up several hours late to retrieve his father. Expecting to get in trouble, he lied to his father about why he was late, saying the garage took longer to repair the car than he expected.

His father recognized the lie, and instead of punishing Arun, punished himself; saying, "There's something wrong in the way I brought you up that didn't give you the confidence to tell me the truth. In order to figure out where I went wrong with you, I'm going to walk home eighteen miles and think about it." His father's self-punishment changed Arun's life forever, inspiring him to travel the globe teaching lessons on peace and non-violence. It's this sort of thoughtful engagement with the people who morally wrong us that the Doctor is trying to teach.

Some events in our lives forever change us, whether those events are caused by people around us or caused by ourselves. We must learn how to respond to being wronged. We must realize that travelling the moral landscape isn't always easy, nor is it always pleasant. We must look for companions that will travel with us on our journeys. But once we begin engaging life properly, and begin working through our own personal moral challenges, we'll find new ways of looking at punishment, justice, revenge, and yes, even forgiveness and self-forgiveness.

Beyond
Everything

6
Religion, Loss, and Afterlife

I'm the Doctor, and I save people.

—TWELFTH DOCTOR, "Flatline," 2014

Whether a person is religious or not, religion strikes a nerve that can tear people apart faster than a black hole sucking in an "impossible planet." Still, even with the contentious nature of religious discussions, it shouldn't be avoided. Religion has the power to provide our lives with meaning and purpose, and though it can inspire us to be mean and evil, it can also inspire us to do great and wonderful things. When it inspires the latter, it mirrors the Doctor's mission to get viewers to see a better way of life and to live it.

Doctor Who's relation to and status as religion has become a hot topic. PBS Idea Channel's video "Is *Doctor Who* a Religion?" provides several reasons for why *Doctor Who* is a religion. It begins by citing Clifford Geertz's claim that religion is a system of symbols that organizes people around a general order of existence (a cosmology), which answers questions about the meaning and purpose of life. The video continues by suggesting that like all world religions, *Doctor Who* provides a cosmology of symbols that organizes its fans in such a way that fills their lives with meaning and motivates them to follow the teachings and lessons of the god-like Doctor.

Similarly, Gladstone's "How *Doctor Who* Became My Religion" claims that *Doctor Who* is religion because it provides the feelings of a relationship with God, a savior from evil, who is a fallible friend who needs us. It's a religious experience that emotionally moves and teaches Gladstone about the nature of the universe. There have even been several books on the religious and mythical themes within *Doctor Who*, the two most notable being Andrew Crome and James F. McGrath's *Time and Relative Dimensions in Faith* and Anthony Burdge, Jessica Burke, and Kristine Larsen's *The Mythological Dimensions of Doctor Who*.

On Doctor Who as a Religion

On a very basic level, religion is a set of human beliefs and practices directed towards the worship of the divine (or the unseen). So, studying religion allows us to learn about ourselves, others, and how we understand the entire universe. In fact, religion is such a deep part of human existence, that many instances of art, history, literature, music, eating habits, violent conflicts, and moral values can't be fully understood without understanding the religious symbols referenced. For instance, *Moby-Dick* is just a boring old book detailing the life of a fisherman, if you have no knowledge of the religious symbolism seen throughout Herman Melville's masterpiece. With an understanding of these symbols, it comes alive with meaning. Even within *Doctor Who*, the Doctor's angelic ascension in "Voyage of the Damned" (2007) takes on a whole new dimension if you're familiar with the story of Jesus of Nazareth's ascension in the Christian scriptures. You don't need a religious background to understand the episode, but it adds extra meaning if you do.

It's this meaning that enriches the lives of so many religious people. The great theologian Paul Tillich described religion as "the ultimate concern." John Hick, another profound theologian, described religion as deemphasizing the self through the seeking of salvation via the divine. Along these same lines, William James refers to religion as belief in an unseen order that challenges us to move towards the supreme good. Finally, in *Hearing the Call*, Nicholas Wolterstorff eloquently describes the "simplicity, sobriety, and measure" of having a relationship with a God who actually loves and suffers with us.

The first thing for us to do is discuss the difference between religion and theology, since they describe two very different things. Religion is about human practice and ritual. It comes from the Latin *religiō*, and is used to describe human conscientiousness and piety towards a deity. Theology, on the other hand, is the study of God—*theos* being Greek for 'God'. So, when we talk of religion the focus is on how humans are reverent towards the divine beings they worship, and has nothing to do with the nature of the deity in itself. All good critical thinkers strive to be clear about the question they want to answer, and realizing that we're only interested in the human practice of worship, not in the nature of what they're worshiping—at least not directly—is key to ensuring we actually answer the question "Is *Doctor*

Who Religion?" and not some other question, like "Is the Doctor God?"

There are many different ways to be religious. This is seen in the fact that there are many different world religions that span the globe (First peoples, African, Judaism, Christianity, Islam, Sikhism, Zoroastrianism, Hinduism, Buddhism, Jainism, Taoism, Confucianism, and among others, Shintoism), and there are several religious traditions unique to a particular geographical area. Within each of these religions is a set of different religious practices. For instance, within Christianity, Catholics and Protestants worship differently, within Protestant denominations, Baptists and Pentecostals worship different, and even particular denominations, like Baptists, have vastly different worship styles. In addition to these historically recognized religions, worldviews like capitalism, communism, being Republican or Democrat, and yes, even television shows like *Doctor Who* are sometimes considered religions.

Simply saying something is a religion doesn't make it one. *Doctor Who* might resemble religion, because of the nature of the show and its fan-base, but in order to be labeled "religion," it must meet certain criteria. Scholars who study comparative religions have attempted to provide a list of criteria of what all religions share. Let's look at two of these lists.

Lewis Hopfe provides the following six characteristics of a world religion. It:

- **features a relationship to the unseen**
- **includes stories of the unseen**
- **contains a set of organized rituals**

- provides an account of afterlife
- provides a code of conduct
- generates large followings

Doctor Who seems to share most of these character-istics. It generates a large following. As this book argues, it provides a general code of conduct, both within the show and within the fan community. It has organized rituals at conventions around the globe, and as I argue in "Why Time Lords Do Not Live Forever," it provides an account of the afterlife.

The two characteristics it might not share with other world religions is that it doesn't seem to feature a rela-tionship with the unseen, nor does it include stories of the unseen. In a broad sense, we could argue that the show's mythos, both in terms of the characters but also of the creation, advocates, detractors, and other contrib-utors to the show, provide a relationship and stories to an unseen, but these are different than typical religious beliefs.

Take, for instance, religious scripture. Most world religions have scripture that informs and enrichers the religion. Followers often base their religious be-liefs and practices on how their scripture describes the unseen. The scripture becomes a conduit in which ad-herents can properly worship. Unless you believe in the divine inspiration of *Doctor Who*, then this doesn't seem to be the focus of the show. *Doctor Who*'s mythos more closely resembles the historical disagreement over the authority, history, and translation of scrip-ture. This sort of disagreement involves an unseen (the unknown history of the scripture), but the unseen is not the divine; it's the historical quirks of producing a meaningful set of documents.

There is, however, another type of relationship with the unseen provided by *Doctor Who*, and that is the relationship it creates between individuals and the fictional character the Doctor. A fictional character is by definition unseen, since it's ultimately a figment in the imagination of an author until being brought to life by an actor or illustrator. This claim is different from the *real* unseen that Hopfe and other religious persons claim to be a characteristic of world religions. A religious person might claim they can't know for certain that their divine exists, that they can't know every aspect of their religious mythos, but their worship is at the very least based on the faith claim that the unseen does exist.

To worship the Doctor is to worship a fictional unseen, and to worship a fiction runs the risk of stripping the religious act of meaning. One might reply that the Doctor represents concepts of goodness and justice, and that it's these concepts that we worship. If that's the case, then the unseen are the concepts, and not the Doctor; which means the Doctor would be the means by which we commune with the unseen, but is not the unseen. Maybe Hopfe's characteristics are too strict.

Ninian Smart, a renowned scholar of comparative religion, provides a different set of characteristics. A religion:

- **contains rituals for participation provides a mythological explanation of the universe**

- **contains doctrinal rules for proper worship**

- **provides ethical standards**

- **creates a social component for human interaction**

- **is experiential, in the sense that participants can in some way experience the divine**

Doctor Who fares better with Smart's list. *Doctor Who* contains rituals, provides a mythos, has internal and external doctrinal rules, provides ethical standards, and creates a social framework of interaction. Does it allow participants to experience the divine? Well, yes and no. As seen in the discussion of Hopfe, it's difficult to say that a fictional character is an actual god, so we wouldn't want to say that *Doctor Who* allows us to experience god-as-the-Doctor. However, if the Doctor (or more generally, *Doctor Who*) presents ultimate truths that allow viewers to experience and better-understand the character and nature of the divine, then yes, it allows viewers to experience the divine indirectly through these truths.

We, then, have a conceptual grounding for the claim that *Doctor Who* is religion. However, the truth of this grounding will depend upon whether we focus on the need for an actual unseen, transcendently divine being, like Hopfe, or on the actions and structures that organize the life of religious persons, like Smart.

Doctor Who as Humanist Religion

If *Doctor Who* is a religion, then maybe it's a type of Humanist religion. 'Humanism' has multiple meanings and implications, but at its heart is the praise of human ability, achievement, and potential. First developed in the Renaissance, its roots can be traced back to earlier philosophies that praise the human ability to reason and self-govern. The Renaissance was fertile ground for Humanism because people had the time, money, knowledge, technology, and leisure to develop human talents and skills beyond what had previously been seen—think Leonardo Da Vinci! Humanism gained momentum during the Enlightenment, when people began looking for answers that didn't require the mystical and the divine. So, no matter the form of Humanism to which you ascribe, the focus will always be human intellect and ability. Everything else detracts from the near-infinite potential of humans.

Because of its emphasis on human ability, Humanism is often considered in opposition to theism, spiritualism, and the supernatural, since such things shift the focus away from humans. There are, however, many types of Humanism. Pragmatic Humanists often believe in God, but reject mysticism in favor of empirical scientific enquiry. They're often deists, because they believe that God created the universe but isn't actively involved in its workings. A second category, secular Humanism can be atheist or deist, but either way, questions of God are of little importance. Science and understanding the secular world are often their main concerns. Spiritual Humanists are often a type of existential theist or spiritualist that focus on the existential fears and anxieties of humanity.

Finally, though not exhaustively, Marxists, existentialists, and naturalists maintain that only what can be seen (or understood through some sort of scientific process) can be known, and instead of asking questions about the unseen, we should focus on the material conditions of humanity and how our decisions make such conditions better or worse. William James, who tried to create a bridge between Humanist empirical inquiry and religious rationalism described Humanism as

> the doctrine that to an unascertainable extent our truths are man-made products too. Human motives sharpen all our questions, human satisfactions lurk in all our answers, all our formulas have a human twist . . . The world is what we make it.

Another helpful quote about Humanism comes from Paul Kurtz, who suggests that Humanism is summed up with the belief that "it's possible to lead a good life and contribute significantly to human welfare and social justice without a belief in theistic religion or benefit of clergy."

Is *Doctor Who* a Humanist religion? It definitely celebrates humans. One of the best examples of the celebration of humans is seen in "Impossible Planet" (2006), when the Tenth Doctor says, "Stand still, I'm going to hug you . . . Humans, absolutely brilliant and completely mad." Other examples are seen in the Eleventh Doctor's command to be "be extraordinary" ("Cold Blood," 2010) and Rose's speech at the end of "The Parting of the Ways" (2005).

It also warns humans of their potential to do evil. It shows us what happens when we fill our lives with hatred (Daleks), or when we try to erase our humanity (Cybermen). Some of the lessons show how greed can ruin your life (Adam in "The Long Game" (2005) and IDW *Prisoners of Time* comic series). One of the most chilling examples of "ordinary" human evil appears in "Midnight" (2008), where the ignorance and stupidity of humans culminates in a competition of who's willing to throw people to their death. Finally, as I argued in

"Philosophy, *Fantastic!*", *Doctor Who* challenges us to see beyond our narrow shortsightedness of greed, hatred, and willful ignorance, and instead, strive for knowledge and wisdom.

Doctor Who definitely presents a Humanist philosophy, but it seems to lack the mystical unseen nature so often associated with religion. Fans derive inspiration and are emotionally moved by the show, some are even obsessed, but it's unclear that they actually *worship* the show—at least not in the way one would worship a transcendent deity. If there were proofs outside of *Doctor Who* (say, from NASA) suggesting the existence of Time Lords, then we might have grounds for claiming that *Doctor Who* is a religion, but without the unseen, it appears to be missing that vital component that would make it a religion.

Such a conclusion is in no way negative. Humanism doesn't have an unseen portion, and Humanist aren't upset. In fact, trying to create a "Humanist religion" by incorporating the worship of something unseen seems to diminish both concepts. It becomes a Humanist position that shifts focus away from human reason and ability to the worship of a non-human authority figure. There are worse things that can happen, but in terms of Humanism, things that detract from human ability go against its basic principles.

Maybe the best approach is to view *Doctor Who* as a middle road between Humanism and religion. Alexander Bertland suggests something similar in "*Doctor Who* as Philosopher and Myth Maker." As Bertland shows, it's easy to think the Doctor always supports Humanist and scientific values, but in fact, he often strikes a balance between both science and myth. What this suggests is that the universe is worse off when we only have either science or myth; and when both work in concert, they enrich our lives, help us recognize truth, and provide meaning. Think of the scene in "Gridlock" (2007), when what seems to be a fairly secular society communes through the singing of old hymns, or in "Snakedance" (1983), when the Doctor encounters a secular and cynical society that must rely on spiritualism in order to combat the Mara.

So, when we watch *Doctor Who*, it teaches important Humanist lessons like the importance of living authentic engaged lives, seeking truth, helping those in need, being fantastic, being extraordinary, and having no regrets, no tears, no anxieties. While at the same time, it fosters a sense that there might be a realm of the unexplained and unseen worthy of worship—that an authentic religious life can be one of the greatest experiences of our human existence.

Benediction

It might surprise some readers, but I don't see *Doctor Who* as a religion, though I understand how others might. I tend to side with Hopfe, emphasizing the need for the "unseen" in religion. Without some sort of unseen, 'religion' feels to be a hollow term that equates with every other ideology. For me, *Doctor Who* is most properly understood as a philosophy—a way of life that promotes a mixture of Humanist and religious values. This doesn't diminish *Doctor Who* in any way. It just shows us that it's different and special.

Maybe the reason so many people want to call *Doctor Who* a religion is because so much of contemporary life lacks meaning, while *Doctor Who* provides an abundance of meaning. In this sense *Doctor Who* is akin to what Rudolf Otto calls "the holy." Have you ever revisited a place you loved to visit as a kid? Do you get a special feeling when you return to that place, as though it is holy or sacred? That's the sort of feeling Otto tries to describe with "the holy." He describes such a feeling as something so good it's beyond good, as though there's a dependence between you and the object that grips and stirs your very being.

Otto's sense of "the holy" is what I experience with *Doctor Who*. It's a powerful feeling that is the closest thing I've ever felt to religious transcendence outside of a religious setting. Yet, the realization that it is fiction—though I wish it weren't—prevents me from describing it as religious. I think 'sacred' and 'holy' are probably good descriptors for the show, and I think others often confuse these feelings with the feelings associated with religion. It's not a bad thing to confuse the two, but as good critical thinkers, we should always try to use the right terms.

Nevertheless, if people want to call it religion, I celebrate their excitement. So much of popular culture, and life itself, is void of meaning and purpose. One of the great things about *Doctor Who* is that it's full of meaning and it provides lessons that show viewers their life has purpose. As long as you're not hurting others, and you're striving to be a better person and create a better world, then all I have to say to you is . . . Allons-y!

Now that we've addressed the issue of *Doctor Who* being religion, let's look at some lessons from *Doctor Who* that are usually associated with religion.

Endings, and Other Depressing Things

I always rip out the last page of a book . . . Then it doesn't have to end. I hate endings!

—ELEVENTH DOCTOR, "The Angels Take Manhattan," 2012

Never let him see the damage. And never ever let him see you age. He doesn't like endings.

—River Song, "The Angels Take Manhattan," 2012

Do you hate endings, and if so, why? Endings are some of the most natural things in the universe. Sunsets end, meals end, songs end, our lives end, and yes, even the longest running sci-fi show must end one day—it's already happened once! Endings can be scary and sad, but should we hate them? The Doctor says he hates endings, so much so that he never reads the end of books. I'm afraid, however, that his claim of hating endings is an example of Rule #1: the Doctor lies. The Doctor, and more generally, *Doctor Who* does NOT hate endings. One of the show's main themes is that things end. The Doctor's life comes to an end every few years, and the time zie shares with his companions usually only lasts a year or so. Sure, these events are sad, but they are not to be hated. *Doctor Who* primarily promotes the acceptance and embracing of endings. Its main lesson is that if we engage endings like we do life, they enrich our existence, provide closure, and give us the opportunity to mature and grow. For some readers, those who've suffered great loss, you're probably thinking "ridiculous," but I hope from exploring *Doctor Who*'s lessons on endings you'll begin to see their value.

The TARDIS Rotation Method

Let's begin by examining an existential explanation for why we might not like endings. Think about your favorite Doctor. When you heard zie was leaving the show, did you find yourself celebrating, or did you find yourself panicking—who are they going to get, you can't replace zir, will it be the same show? This is natural. We become accustomed to things, and when we find something we like, we don't want it to end. When the Ninth Doctor regenerated into the Tenth, I said, "I just don't know if I'm going to like this new guy." This "new guy" was David Tennant, and by the middle of his first season, he'd blown me away too.

Many are still experiencing this phenomenon with Jodie Whittaker's incarnation. This is how life and endings typically work. Something ends, something new is introduced, and we can't imagine liking this new thing. We're happy and comfortable with the old, but after a period of time we come to love the new things just as much, if not more, than the old. We must learn to recognize that things change and we must learn to become comfortable with this change.

Yet, change remains scary. The Danish philosopher Søren Kierkegaard (1813–1855) discusses such a fear with what he calls the aesthetic life. The aesthetic life is a life concerned only with beauty and its resulting pleasure. As Kierkegaard notes, beauty and pleasure are among some of the most short-lived events in our lives. Most of life is working, paying bills, and if you're lucky, having a companion to share your life with. Because of this, the aesthetic life is filled with the dread that pleasure will come to an end. To avoid pleasure's end, Kierkegaard suggests that the aesthetic life must use what he calls "the rotation method," where you constantly change and replace pleasures in the hope of keeping things fresh and new.

Imagine you love *Doctor Who*, but you only have one episode—no books, magazines, or any sort of other *Doctor Who* paraphernalia. How long will it take before you get tired of your one episode? If it's hard to imagine such a thing, imagine eating the same food every day. Eventually, you're going to get tired of it. The excitement and enjoyment of the thing, whether it's food or your favorite TV show, begins to wear off. To avoid this happening, you need to watch other episodes, or other TV shows, or try eating different things. If you don't use the rotation method, then you'll quickly grow to despise the thing you once loved. Kierkegaard warns, however, that even with the rotation method, the life of the aesthetic contains an ever-present threat of boredom and monotony.

In order to avoid such a life, *Doctor Who* suggests we fill our lives with meaning and purpose. It doesn't mean we ignore or avoid pleasurable things in life, but we shouldn't make those things the center of our lives. We must recognize that pleasures are apt to end, and that if the only thing of meaning in our life is pleasure, we've set ourselves up for failure. Instead, we should focus our lives on things that are meaningful and long-lasting. Such things typically carry with them their own set of pleasures. When we're lucky enough to have pleasure in our life, we shouldn't take it for granted.

The Doctor teaches that we must learn to recognize and enjoy each moment, realizing that each one only lasts a mere fraction of second, and that we never know what the next moment will bring. Instead of worrying about losing that one precious moment, or worrying about what the future might bring, we must learn to be comfortable in and take advantage of the now. We delight in what is, and ignore what was or what could be. This is a difficult lesson that few master, but the more we take a realistic approach to pleasure, and learn to focus on things that are long-lasting and meaningful, the more likely we are to flourish. When we take this approach to life, endings have no power over us. Of course, even for those who are successful at this, the fear of death is often the most difficult to overcome.

Life, Death, Afterlife

One of humanity's greatest fears is our mortality. As I note in "Why Time Lords Do Not Live Forever," one of the most common features of religion is that it provides an account of what happens when you die. Some stories of afterlife are more complicated that others, some are pleasant, and some are to be avoided at all costs, but each account addresses a deep-rooted fear humans have about their mortal existence. A result of this fear is that death becomes the enemy. It's the great unknown, and it appears to rob us of this plane of existence, but is death really the enemy?

Philosophy is one of the few departments of life that isn't afraid to talk about death. In Plato's dialogue *Phaedo*, Socrates claims that one of philosophy's greatest virtues is that it prepares us for death. What Socrates means is that philosophy makes us approach death in a critical and logical way, separating what reason tells us from what our fearful imagination says.

When we rationally consider death, Socrates argues that there's nothing to fear. In Plato's *Apology*, upon receiving his death sentence, Socrates argues that death is either something or nothing. If it's something, then it should resemble in some way the process of change we currently experience, except that it will be populated by people who died before us. So, when we die we get to hang out with everyone who preceded us in death. If it's nothing, then death is like taking an eternal nap, which unless you think getting a little extra shut-eye is bad, you shouldn't fear. Based on these two possibilities, which are both positive, death is nothing to fear.

In the previously mentioned *Phaedo*, Plato uses the voice of Socrates to offer a slightly different account of death. In the dialogue, Socrates builds off an argument made in the *Meno* (that the soul exists prior to our life on Earth) to argue that the soul is immortal. With knowledge of the soul's immortality, we should direct our lives towards The Good (what later theologians describe as God), using reason and wisdom to focus on ultimate reality, while avoiding the distractions and ignorance of earthly physical pleasures.

It's always difficult talking about death with the Doctor, since zie doesn't die. Yet, *Doctor Who* does provide an account of the afterlife, though like Plato's two dialogues, they differ slightly. As I argue in "Why Time Lords Do Not Live Forever," the Classic series suggests that there's no subjective afterlife, in the sense that when a person dies they continue having new subjective experiences similar to the ones they had while alive. Instead, the Classic series suggests that at some point subjective life simply comes to an end, and that it's perverse to want to be immortal. Look at what happens to Lord Borusa in "The Five Doctors" (1983). His desire to be immortal leads him to kidnap and kill innocent people, and he's punished by being made immortal, as a living stone figure on Rassilon's tomb. The Master seeks immortality, and it only leads to insanity, destruction, and most often death. "The Three Doctors" (1972–73) provides us with one of the most shocking examples of immortality, Lord Omega. Omega's immortality, trapped within the antimatter universe, produced a hatred and resentment that ate away every other part of himself, leaving only his will to destroy.

Instead of a subjective experience, the Classic series suggests a type of objective immortality (at least for Time Lords), where all of the thoughts and experiences of each Time Lord is perfectly preserved in the Amplified Panatropic Computer Network known as the Matrix. Time Lords, then, have a type of immortality, but it's not a personal immortality. Rather, it's an immortality that allows for their experiences to be perfectly preserved for all future generations.

Similar to the Matrix, the New series suggests that it's possible to capture the mental experiences of individuals. As seen in "Dark Water" and "Death in Heaven" (2014), Missy uses Time Lord technology to upload the mental data of everyone who dies. However, these two episodes suggest that within the Nethersphere individuals continue to have subjective experiences, similar to what happens to River Song in "Forest of the Dead" (2008).

So, what we end up with is exactly what Socrates suggested. Either death leads to a nothingness similar to the Classic series Matrix, or it leads to change, as illustrated by the Nethersphere in the New series. Which one is right? We probably won't ever know until we die, but regardless, as Socrates suggests, neither is to be feared.

Just This Time Everyone . . . Dies

For such a life-affirming show, *Doctor Who* has a lot of death. The Doctor isn't afraid of death. It's a natural end of our human existence. What's more, *Doctor Who* often gives us stories of heroes engaged in life-and-death struggles, and sometimes these heroes sacrifice their lives in order to save others. Jabe gives her life to save everyone on the space station Platform One ("The End of the World," 2005). Harriet Jones, Prime Minister (yes, we know who you are), saves the universe in "Stolen Earth" (2008), but only by sacrificing her life in order to "call" the Doctor. Finally, Donna Noble sacrifices her life in "Turn Left" (2008), in order to preserve a timeline where the Doctor lives and is able to continue saving the universe.

All of these examples are what Aristotle would call acts of courage. They are examples of people making tough moral decisions in the face of death. Instead of being a coward, or acting foolishly, they risked their lives in the face of danger, and died saving others. For many, there's not much in life nobler than giving your life to save others.

In his *Nicomachean Ethics*, Aristotle argues that life is one long test of being courageous. Aristotle maintains that we should use our impending death as the basis for acting and making the best of this life. As the Doctor suggests at the conclusion of "The End of the World," instead of spending our time worrying about asteroids, politics, disasters, and death, we should make the best of our life on Earth by living courageously in the face of these facts of human existence. So, for Aristotle, death brings value to life. Without death, the fear is that there would be no motive to act, unless you just really wanted to do something. If we are immortal, then we could waste this life and hope for the best in the next. Death, however, puts this life in perspective, and inspires us to make the best of the time we have on Earth.

If you share Aristotle's outlook on life and death, then death isn't the worst thing that can happen to a person. As John Hardwig discusses in his book *Is There a Duty to Die?*, there are certain things, like unbearable pain and suffering, and causing others to suffer and die, which are worse than death. The New series seems to support Aristotle and Hardwig. For example, Amy's decision to commit suicide in "Amy's Choice" (2010) illustrates that, for her, the loss of a close loved one is worse than death. The Doctor's willingness to go along with Amy implies that he agrees. Another example occurs in "The Angels Take Manhattan" (2012), when Amy and Rory decide to commit suicide instead of living in a world of continual suffering.

In both of these examples, everyone ends up surviving, but not every episode has such a "happy" ending. In one of the most shocking examples of a character choosing death over life, in a non-heroic way, is Adelaide Brooke in "The Waters of Mars" (2009). In an attempt to defy the Tenth Doctor's "Time Lord Victorious," Adelaide kills herself. She claims that the Time Lord Victorious is wrong, and that instead of living in such a world, she ends her life. No matter their reasons or the story's outcome, these characters preferred death over continued existence, which suggests that death isn't the worst thing that can happen in this life.

I'm in no way suggesting that *Doctor Who* supports suicide, and I would plead with anyone who's had suicidal thoughts to seek help. But it does support the idea that death isn't the worst thing that can happen to a person. Based on what we've just discussed, death is simply an end that should not be feared. It's not even the worst thing that can happen to us. Instead, death should motivate us to make the best of the life we have, and should teach us that it takes courage to risk our lives in the face of death. As Aristotle and the Doctor suggest, choosing to live our lives is an act of courage that rids death of any power it might have over us.

The End of Birth

Death isn't the only ending *Doctor Who* is interested in exploring. Birth, which is most often celebrated as the beginning of life, can be one of the most devastating ends for some couples. During "Asylum of the Daleks" (2012), viewers discover that Amy and Rory have separated due to their inability to conceive a child. For the Ponds, and for all real-life couples who can't conceive, the inability to produce a child is one of the most devastating ends imaginable.

The ability to bear children is one of the oldest and most natural worries of humans. Generally speaking, humans are biologically driven to reproduce. Historically, a woman's ability to bear children has often been closely associated with her value in society, and her inability sometimes seen as a curse. Spend some time reading ancient texts, like the Hebrew scriptures, and you'll see how important it was that a woman be able to bear children. Contemporary studies have shown that it's most often the man who is infertile, but the stigma still exists in some areas and families that a barren woman is "less than" one who's able to produce children.

The Doctor doesn't deal directly with these social biases, but we know he's against anything that arbitrarily devalues any sort of life, which is what happens when we associate a person's value to some arbitrary ability—even if that ability is the ability to bear children. Nevertheless, *Doctor Who* does show the devastating effect of not being able to conceive children. In addition to "Asylum of the Daleks," the episode "The Girl Who Waited" (2011) gives viewers a glimpse into the anger and resentment that can develop as a result of wanting and waiting. Just as the years waiting on Rory and the Doctor made Amy bitter, waiting on having a child can not only tear couples apart but it can cause individuals to question their own purpose and existence. For those who've never experienced such anguish, it sounds strange and it's hard to empathize, but *Doctor Who* provides viewers with a glimpse inside the pain of couples and individuals who've suffered this devastating end.

What lesson does *Doctor Who* have for us who can't have children? As always, it tells us not to give up. It tells us to refocus our energies, to re-examine our priorities, and to develop new strategies for how to "have children." It teaches that you can get involved in mentoring, teaching, fostering, adopting, and being an advocate for children. It doesn't teach us that there will never be any heart-wrenching pain when you see families doing things you'll never be able to do, but it teaches us that we can use that pain to grow and mature. We can help others, especially the millions of children that so desperately need and want someone to unconditionally love them, who need someone to take them on their journey through space and time. In other words, it teaches us to reinterpret one end into a new beginning, focused on what we can do, not on what we can't.

The Doctor's End

Courage isn't just a matter of not being frightened, you know. It's being afraid and doing what you have to do anyway.

—THIRD DOCTOR, "Planet of the Daleks," 1973

Too often with endings we focus on what's lost, but *Doctor Who* teaches viewers to focus on what can be, on using endings to make ourselves better persons. Nothing illustrates this principle as nicely as the Doctor's death and regeneration. In "The Tenth Planet" (1966) the Doctor's "body wears thin" saving the universe. In other words, he worked himself to death helping others. The Cybermen were simply the final straw. Did he quit? No. He became more energetic, and as a result of his increasing activity saving the universe, he winds up getting punished by the Time Lords for "meddling" ("The War Games," 1969). Did he stop meddling, or just give up trying to save the universe? No. He meddled even more.

The Third Doctor's tenure came to an end when his greed for knowledge ended in a massive dose of radiation ("Planet of the Spiders," 1974). He learned his lesson, and sat out on a new adventure as a "scarfy" artist and philosopher. His commitment to helping others never ceased, and the Fourth Doctor's end occurs when he falls to his death protecting the universe from the Master ("Logopolis," 1981). This doesn't deter him one bit, for in the very next episode the Fifth Doctor is fighting the Master again ("Castrovalva," 1982). The Doctor might change clothing, his looks, and his character, but as R. Alan Siler notes in "Magnetic North," the Doctor's magnetic north—the direction he always points—is to be good and to help those in need. So, when the Fifth Doctor's end comes, we find him again sacrificing his life for a friend ("Caves of Androzani," 1984).

The Sixth Doctor hits the universe with a little more energy and a lot more color than his predecessors, and his commitment to save the universe is just as brilliant. He's again put on trial for "meddling" ("The Trial of a Time Lord," 1986), and by the time it's all said and done, it's up to the Seventh Doctor to fight the good fight. The Seventh Doctor's end comes as a result of gang violence and human error (*Doctor Who: TV Movie*), but he returns as passionate and debonair as ever. Like Socrates drinking his hemlock, the Eighth Doctor's end is a self-administered action designed to create a "Doctor" capable of ending the Time War ("The Night of the Doctor," 2013). The War Doctor wears thin after preventing the genocide of the Time Lords ("The Day of the Doctor"). The Ninth ends by saving his friend Rose ("The Parting of the Ways," 2005). The Tenth ends by saving his friend Wilfred ("The End of Time," 2009–2010). The Eleventh ends saving the town of Christmas ("The Time of the Doctor," 2013). The Twelfth Doctor ends protecting friends and innocents ("The Doctor Falls," 2017). We don't know what will happen when the

Thirteenth Doctor's tenure comes to an end, but based on everything we've seen for the past fifty years, the Doctor will stay true to zirs "magnetic north," carry on learning from endings, and doing what zie has always done: take care of the universe.

Each ending brings us an opportunity for something new. It shows us what's important and it helps refocus our lives. Take, for instance, the Eleventh Doctor's final monologue in "The Day of the Doctor" (2013):

> Clara sometimes asks me if I dream. "Of course I dream," I tell her, "Everybody dreams." "But what do you dream about?" she'll ask. "The same thing everybody dreams about," I tell her, "I dream about where I'm going." She always laughs at that. "But you're not going anywhere, you're just wandering about." That's not true. Not anymore. I have a new destination. My journey is the same as yours the same as anyone's. It's taken me so many years, so many lifetimes, but at last, I know where I'm going, where I've always been going. Home . . . the long way round.

If the Doctor's correct, then we're all heading "home." Home isn't necessarily that building where you keep your stuff, with all those rooms for sleeping. No, home is where you feel most comfortable. It's an accomplishment of hard work and dedication. Home is the safest place for you to dream and reflect upon what's important. So, where is your "home"? For the Doctor, it's a return to helping those in need, and sure he's still looking for Gallifrey, but more importantly, he's looking for meaning and peace. And like any good flâneur, he's going to take the long way to get there.

One of the most interesting aspects of "The Day of the Doctor" is what appears to be a hint about the

Doctor's "home." If the Curator is truly the Fourth Doctor, then we gain insight into the true character of the Doctor. A curator is a caretaker of important things, things that would otherwise be lost or destroyed. With the Curator and the Doctor side-by-side, the Doctor's life as "curator" of the universe comes in sharp relief. By understanding them as dual illustrations of the Doctor's true nature, the dialogue between them takes on a new level of meaning:

> ELEVENTH DOCTOR: I could retire and be the curator of this place.
>
> CURATOR: You know, I really think you might.
>
> ELEVENTH DOCTOR: I never forget a face.
>
> CURATOR: I know you don't, and in years to come you might find yourself revisiting a few . . . but just the old favorites . . . eh? You were curious about this painting, I think. I acquired it in remarkable circumstances. What do you make of the title?
>
> ELEVENTH DOCTOR: Which title? There's two: "No More" or "Gallifrey Falls."
>
> CURATOR: No, that's where everybody is wrong. It's all one title, "Gallifrey Falls, No More." Now, what would you think that means, eh?
>
> ELEVENTH DOCTOR: If Gallifrey didn't fall, it worked, it's still out there.
>
> CURATOR: I'm only a humble curator, I'm sure I wouldn't know.
>
> ELEVENTH DOCTOR: Then, where is it?
>
> CURATOR: Where is it, indeed? Lost. Shh! Perhaps, things do get lost, you know. Now, you must excuse me, you have a lot to do.

ELEVENTH DOCTOR: Do I? Is that what I'm supposed to do? Go looking for Gallifrey?

CURATOR: It's entirely up to you. Your choice, eh? I can only tell you what I would do, if I were you. If I were you . . . Oh, if I were you. Or, perhaps I was you. Or, perhaps you are me—congratulations! Or, perhaps it doesn't matter either way. Who Knows? [touching his hand to his nose] Who knows?

The Curator's last few cryptic words suggest they're the same, and that the heart and soul of the Doctor—his "home"—will always be to take care of the universe, no matter what endings try to get in his way.

Are we courageous enough to learn this lesson and to do the same? If we are, then we must learn to embrace endings. It doesn't mean we have to enjoy them, and that we can't grieve endings, but we must view them in proper perspective. We must see that every ending creates the possibility for a new beginning, and if we're prepared and courageous (no matter how scared we are), we can take advantage of each and every ending life throws our way to make all time and space a better place.

7
Knowledge, Space, and Time

There is something about the type of imagination that powers *Doctor Who* that sweeps up viewers and inspires them in unexpected ways. Something about its mix of the fantastic and the mundane, the far-flung with the domestic, that is unlike anything else.

—DAVID TENNANT

You can't have a book on *Doctor Who* without discussing space and time, what physicists call spacetime. In addition to being the basis of much of the Doctor's timey wimey adventures, spacetime gives us insights into the universe's true reality.

Spacetime Reality

We humans are good with space. From the time we're little babies, we're learning how to navigate it. Yeah, we run into some walls, and our depth-perception takes many months to develop, but after a few years of life, we've mastered space. In fact, I doubt that you spend more than a few seconds a day (if that much) thinking of space. You just move around, go where you want, and hopefully have fun doing it.

Time is another matter altogether. Sure, we have fancy watches and phones that give us "the time," but we never actually observe time. In fact, because it takes several milliseconds for our brains to process events, we never actually perceive the present. There are those who have finely-tuned perceptual skills that come close to perceiving the present, like baseball batters and fighter pilots, but for the most part, our "present" is always just out of our perceptual reaches. So, in a weird way, our perception of the world around us is a type of time travel, though not the cool kind we see in *Doctor Who*.

Even though time seems so different from space, our theories about time generally fail to explain why they're different. We easily move backwards, forwards, and around in space, why not backwards and forwards in time? Unless you're watching the *Red Dwarf* episode "Backwards," time only moves forward from past to present. This forward movement of time is called time's arrow; and even though it's the only way in which humans perceive reality, there are no definite answers for why time moves in one direction.

As Joel Lebowitz asks in "Time's Arrow and Boltzmann's Entropy," "If the laws of nature permit all processes to be run backwards in time, why don't we observe them doing so?" Why don't we ever see an egg uncrack or a glass un-shatter? Why do we remember the past and not the future? With what we know about reality, we should have access to the past and future, just as we have access to the space that surrounds us. Let's see how *Doctor Who* sheds light on any of these questions.

We know that the Doctor travels through all space-time, so our theory of spacetime must capture this phenomenon. As noted by Lebowitz, Presentism maintains that only the present is real, which means the past and future don't physically exist. We can't know the future, because it hasn't happened, and the only access we have to the past is our memories, or historical accounts from others. So, for *Doctor Who*, Presentism can't be correct.

As an alternative, the block universe theory maintains that the past and future exist, and that the present is only an individual's particular viewing of the now. If true, then just as we move around in space, we should be able to move around in time. To quote Lebowitz, "*now* is dependent on one's viewpoint in much the same way that *here* is," and the idea that only the present exists is an illusion. Block theory is definitely supported by *Doctor Who*, and gives us the ability to explain how the TARDIS travels through spacetime—it accesses a time vortex to transcend our human perceptual capacities, in order to travel to past and future events that are impossible with our normal human abilities.

Time-travel, therefore, is possible, but how are we to get there? We need a TARDIS, but can a TARDIS exist? The answer seems to be "Yes, sort of." In *More Doctor Who and Philosophy*, Benjamin Tippet and David Tsang show how building a TARDIS is possible, given the right theory of spacetime. A block theory of spacetime works, but there are other limitations. As a bubble of spacetime geometry, based on our current understanding of physics, the TARDIS would only be able to travel in a circle, and it would require exotic matter that is "gravitationally repulsive and would need to move faster than light." Current theories, however, maintain that objects can't travel faster than the speed of light. If they were to travel faster, we'd have to rewrite our physics. As if that weren't enough, other problems include the possibility that anyone traveling in such a bubble would become antimatter. If you think that sounds fun, consider what happens with Omega in "Arc of Infinity" (1983)—he threatens to explode and destroy the universe.

Even though Tippet and Tsang are extremely bright, they aren't Time Lords, so we should cut them some slack for not having all of the answers. As Massimo Pigliucci discusses in *More Doctor Who and Philosophy*, and throughout several other wonderful books, time travel is beyond complex. For a taste of its difficulty, search the Internet for "Top Ten Theories of the Universe." Instead of going down the wormhole of these theories, let us move forward with the idea that time travel and at least the concept of a TARDIS is possible.

With these two ideas in mind, we can say the following about time: 1. time can be re-written; 2. fixed points in time can't be rewritten; 3. knowledge of our future creates a fixed point; and 4. changing your own timeline should be avoided. If you watch *Doctor Who* long enough, you'll find examples where sometimes these four rules are true, while also finding times when they are violated. With the Eleventh and Twelfth Doctors, Steven Moffat delighted in making the Doctor uphold and violate all four. One minute the Doctor can't avoid Trenzalore, the other minute he's preventing the genocide of Time Lords in the Time War. He can't save Clara, then he saves her.

What are we to say? In "What the Doctor Can and Can't Change," Audrey Delamont examines these four possibilities and concludes that *Doctor Who* simply provides us with contradictory answers. To be honest, it's these conundrums that make it fun and keep us coming back for more. Stephen Felder sums up a Whovian view of time like this:

> Each "present" is a future that goes into the past by passing through our experience of it. There isn't a succession of presents, but a perduring, living present, and this present is, in some sense, what each of us like to call "me." These me's are what some scholars call, "the subject," and they intertwine in this perduring because "time is the subject, and the subject is time."
>
> Time is us, and we are time. In this sense, we're all Time Lords. ("Time Lords Are Us")

Learning the Lingo

In the early 1990s I used to dress up as the Doctor for Halloween, and no one knew who I was supposed to be. Since I typically wore a scarf, or an old checkered jacket, they'd often say, "Did you just fly in from the alps?" I would just shake my head, and say, "No, I'm a different kind of doctor—the Doctor!" They still didn't understand.

There are many senses of the term 'know'. I might know you from a convention, or I can know how to play guitar, or I can know that the Doctor is from Gallifrey. The last type of knowledge is called "propositional knowledge," and is the most prominent type of knowledge examined by epistemologists (philosophers who specialize in knowledge). Since the object of propositional knowledge is a proposition (meaning it's either true or false), epistemologists can clearly examine what is said, in order to determine if it is, or if it can be knowable.

To better understand knowledge, we must separate it from belief. First, as Kevin McCain notes in *The Nature of Scientific Knowledge*, knowledge requires belief. You can't know the Doctor is a Time Lord, if you don't have a belief that the Doctor's a Time Lord. However, belief doesn't imply knowledge. I can believe that Cybermen are on their way to invade Earth, but without some sort of further evidence, I can't say I know it. My belief that Cybermen are coming, whether a desire or fear, is mere opinion.

Not all belief is mere opinion, for belief can be grounded in factual occurrences that provide support for my belief. For instance, I can believe *Doctor Who* will be renewed next season, and though I can't know it with any certainty until it is actually renewed, due to its track record of being renewed, my belief is stronger than mere opinion. It's similar to physicians who use their knowledge of medicine and healing to form a belief about sickness. We might incorrectly refer to it as a "medical opinion," but a physician's diagnosis of my physical state is much stronger than my unfounded desire/fear that the Cybermen are coming.

Second, 'knowledge' implies truth, while 'belief' does not. When I say "I know the Doctor exists," I'm making a claim that implies I both have a belief about the Doctor and that it is true. Before discussing how something gains the status of truth, let's look a little closer at my claim to believe the Doctor exists. There are two ways in which you might believe something. I can believe *that* the Doctor exists, which means I have a certain mental state or opinion that there's an actual time-travelling alien who busies zirself saving the universe, or I can believe *in* the Doctor, which means I believe in what the Doctor stands for and represents. Again, as pointed out by McCain, knowledge requires "belief that," not "belief in." I can believe in many things related to the Doctor's character without actually believing that a Time Travelling alien actually exists.

There's a part of me that hopes the belief that the Doctor exists is true, but I actually believe in the Doctor. Such a belief is what David Holley calls "life-orienting," because it shapes my life, and as a result, it's easy for me to *know* my belief in the Doctor is true. My life is influenced by how I watch and interpret the show, and because this belief is central to who I am, I often make knowledge claims regarding *Doctor Who*. The book you're currently holding in your hands is full of them. Regardless of my belief about the Doctor, when I make a knowledge claim I'm asserting that I have good evidence for why it is true. I'm saying more than just "It's my opinion," I'm suggesting I can offer good reasons as "proof" for my belief. Epistemology refers to this "proof" as justification and/or warrant.

The Proof of Justification

Imagine you're the Doctor's companion, and he runs off to get something from zirs TARDIS. Of course, being a companion, you strike up a conversation with some seedy looking bald guy in a toga, who calls himself Socrates. While talking, he asks, "What is knowledge?" After thinking, you respond, "It's whatever I see." This might at first seem like a good answer, but there are three reasons why it isn't.

First, knowledge can't be mere seeing, since such an answer implies when we close our eyes we become ignorant. Second, and more importantly, there are many things we can't see (unless we write them out!), yet we know, for instance, that 2 + 2 = 4. Finally, our vision might be mistaken. Imagine you look off in the distance, see someone who resembles the Doctor, and say, "See, there's the Doctor returning from the TARDIS." However, when the figure gets closer it becomes clear that it was someone else with impeccable style heading your direction. These three reasons show that knowledge must be something else.

Since seeing and perceiving play such fundamental roles in the way we know the world, adding something to them might provide a justification for knowledge. One thing that we might add is a judgment about what we perceive. If you put your thumb in front of your eye, it will look much bigger than most of your surroundings: It will cover other people's heads, the sun, and even a Dalek off in the distance. Your perception suggests your thumb is bigger, but your judgment (your reason) tells you it's an illusion. Such judgment might save your life in the occurrence of a real Dalek heading your way—run!

Judgment (often seen as a kind of belief), then, plays some role in knowledge, especially if the judgement is true. Instead of haphazardly claiming "the Doctor is approaching," because the person resembles the Doctor and you know zie is on the way back from the TARDIS, careful critical thinkers will withhold judgment until zie is closer, so they can be certain they

KNOW zie is coming. In this way, judgment helps ensure knowledge.

The main question now is, does knowledge require certainty? If you say you know the answer to 2 + 2, then you know it with certainty that it's 4. You know it so well, you could even demonstrate it to others. According to Socrates, in Plato's dialogue *Meno*, your ability to demonstrate proves you know what you say you know; that's why teachers give so many tests.

Demonstration and proof, however, come in many different forms. If you want to prove that "all bachelors are unmarried men," you need only ponder the concept of man (married or unmarried male) and bachelor (a man who has never been married) to determine whether it's true. By definition, it is true, since unmarried men are either bachelors or widowers—married men can never be bachelors. On the other hand, if you want to prove that your thumb is smaller than a Dalek, you will have walk up to the Dalek and compare the two—though it might be the last thing you do. Within this explanation, however, lies the problem. Even with the best of judgments, we can still be wrong. Deductive truths, like mathematics, geometry and logic can be known and demonstrated with certainty, but inductive truths, like comparing your thumb's size to a Dalek, lack any such certainty.

The Trouble with a Logical TARDIS

For a long time, most philosophers agreed that knowledge is justified true belief. But then in 1963, the philosopher Edmund Gettier published an article titled " Is Justified True Belief Knowledge?" Gettier's first argument goes something like this: Imagine the Doctor is going to pick his new companion today, and it's come down to you and Bill. From your snooping, you develop excellent reasons for thinking that Bill will be the next companion—you heard the Doctor say that it will be Bill, Bill told you that she would be the next companion, and so on. Since you know that Bill has a blue jean jacket, and you have excellent reason to think that she will be the next companion, you correctly reason that the next companion will have a blue jean jacket. In other words, you have a justified true belief that the next companion will have a blue jean jacket.

Here comes the fun part. Imagine further that you, in fact, own a blue jean jacket, but you have forgotten about it, and the Doctor plans on picking you instead of Bill. It turns out that you are wrong about Bill being the next companion, you are the next companion! But, as it happens your belief that the next companion has a blue jean jacket is true because you have a blue jean jacket. So, your belief that the next companion has a blue jean jacket is both justified (you have good reason to believe it) and true, but it isn't knowledge. You didn't "know" that the next companion will have a blue jean jacket, even though it's a justified true belief. As a result, we've shown that justified true beliefs don't guarantee certain knowledge. A sad state of affairs, indeed, if you wish knowledge to be certain!

Instead of jettisoning knowledge altogether, it's wiser to reject the requirement that knowledge be certain. In fact, since Gettier, many epistemologists have offered accounts of justification designed to show we can have knowledge without certainty, focusing instead on what conditions must be met for knowledge to be warranted.

Rebuilding the Universe's Knowledge

René Descartes (1596–1650) famously argued, "I think, therefore, I am." With this argument, Descartes shows that we, as thinking things, exist beyond any sort of doubt. Even if everything in existence is doubted (the senses, the physical world, and even mathematics), there must be something doing the doubting (and therefore thinking). This doubting occurs as an idea in my mind, and to have ideas means there must be some thinking thing having those ideas. I, therefore, know that, as a thinking thing, I must exist.

Descartes's argument still influences contemporary society, and can be seen in several *Doctor Who* episodes, such as "The Last Christmas" (2014), where the characters know they exist, but can't decide which external existence is real. Descartes is important for our purposes for two reasons. First, he made certainty the goal of knowledge, and second, he is a Classical Foundationalist. As a Classical Foundationalist, he maintains that knowledge is justified by having a belief (or set of beliefs) not justified by other beliefs. "I think, therefore, I am" (often called the Cogito, since the Latin for 'I think, therefore I am" is 'Cogito, ergo sum') is one such belief. The Cogito requires no further beliefs to be true, so it serves as a foundation for the rest of knowledge. To deny the Cogito, serves only to justify it further; for to have a belief requires a thinking thing to have a belief about denying a belief.

That seems obvious enough, but Descartes's foundationalism has been challenged by many philosophers over the centuries.

David Hume (1711–1776) distinguished between inductive and deductive reasoning, and argued that knowledge based on experience can only be known by induction. Many of the beliefs we hold to be true—the sun will rise in the east, my car will start, *Doctor Who* will be renewed for another season—can't be known with certainty. Nature can always change, cars break, and TV executives make stupid decisions. However, if we're careful with the claims and assumptions we make, beliefs can be true with a high degree of probability. So, until *Doctor Who* shows signs of being canceled, my belief in its renewal is strong.

Finally, Thomas Reid (1710–1796) suggested that we dispense with the Cartesian "way of ideas" that separates the mind from the world implied by the Cogito, and instead, focus on the direct perception of the external world. According to Reid, Descartes's insistence on the existence of a thinking thing (a self or consciousness) that only perceives the world via its perception of ideas in the mind leads to a skepticism of the external world's existence. Reid's arguments for how it is possible to perceive the world directly will suggest an approach to epistemology that allows for knowledge to result from our natural perception and engagement with the world. This approach, then, allows for beliefs justified by reliable belief-generating devices, like the senses, and this concept is known as reliabilism.

Justification Regenerated

Our main question remains, what justifies belief, thereby, making it knowledge? Based directly or indirectly on the work of the philosophers just examined (and many others), the past forty years offer some intriguing answers.

Beginning with the work of William Alston in the 1970s, foundationalism underwent a regeneration of its own. Addressing the criticism of arbitrary beliefs, in "Two Types of Foundationalism," Alston argues for a foundationalism, similar to Reid's work, based on our perception and engagement with the world. For Alston, we have a certain level of knowledge that occurs simply as a result of our biological connection to our surroundings. As a result, there are two "levels" of knowledge: a. a lower level that occurs immediately through perception; and b. a higher level that occurs when we reflect upon our ideas or try to justify why we know something to be true. To illustrate, imagine you see the TARDIS as you walk through the park. How do you know that you're seeing the TARDIS? Well, you know it because you're actually perceiving it. Assuming you're not sick, hallucinating, or on a movie set, your perceptual abilities reliably give you information about the world, and in this instance they tell you that you're seeing the TARDIS. Do you know this with certainty? No. But if you senses are reliable, then Alston maintains that you have an immediate belief that counts as knowledge, at least on a lower level.

Not all knowledge occurs on this lower level. Humans have the ability to reflect on their beliefs, and if needed, provide justifications. The ability and need to justify beliefs illustrates how humans also have a higher level of knowledge. Seeing the TARDIS is a pretty shocking event, so much so that if it were to occur, your mind would probably shift instantly into a higher level or reasoning. You would investigate to see if it were the genuine article or a knock off. The same thing would happen, if someone asked "how do you know you saw the TARDIS?" Any time you reflect on a belief or provide justifications for a belief, you're using higher level epistemic reasoning.

Alston's discussion of levels of knowledge illustrates the difference between *being* justified and *showing* that one is justified. In cases where you properly perceive something, you are justified by the process of perception. When you reflect, or your belief is challenged, you are justified by the process of proving (i.e. showing) your belief to yourself or others.

In a general way, allowing for a lower level of knowledge supports the conception of reality shown in *Doctor Who*. If only those capable of higher level reasoning can be said to have knowledge, then we must doubt the possibility of children, animals, adults with cognitive disabilities, and a whole host of aliens having knowledge. Any being incapable of providing justifications for their beliefs must be said to lack knowledge, and this inability would influence their moral status, because it implies an inferiority to those who are capable of higher level reasoning. The Doctor is continually giving creatures the benefit of doubt, respecting their ability to understand and know what is best for them. Even when the Doctor encounters a group who is unwilling to listen to zirs pleas, zie uses methods to help them understand.

Alston's foundationalism addresses the criticism of Classical Foundationalism that foundational beliefs are arbitrary by grounding beliefs in the non-arbitrary belief-generating process of our senses. Since certainty is too much to ask in terms of justification, reliabilism provides strong support for how we know certain things and why we know them.

Some worry that reliabilism is too weak to support a rich epistemology. For instance, Keith Lehrer suggests that reliabilism only allows for the incorporation of information, not knowledge, and he uses the example of Mr. Truetemp to illustrate. Without knowing, Mr. Truetemp has a device implanted in his head that allows him to get accurate temperature readings. The device allows him to have reliable information about the external temperature transferred directly from the device to his "belief center," without any further conscious consideration on his part. Mr. Truetemp "just knows" the temperature without thinking, and he's incapable of explaining how he has this information. Lehrer suggests that such an account of knowledge is flawed because Mr. Truetemp does not have knowledge, he just has information about the temperature. He "knows" the temperature, like an automated door "knows" someone is entering the building.

Mr. Truetemp kind of sounds like a character the Doctor might help on one of zirs adventures, and even though many take him to show reliability isn't sufficient for knowledge, reliabilists disagree. For a reliabilist, Lehrer commits a level confusion by requiring that Mr. Truetemp go beyond *being* justified by his perception to *showing* why he is justified in knowing the temperature. Mr. Truetemp's belief is justified by the process of how he comes to have the belief, not by being able to give reasons for why he has the belief. If I see a Judoon coming at me with a gun, I'm justified in my belief that he's coming at me, even if I can't explain the visual process of perception. If I could, then my belief would be that much stronger; but to know and react to the oncoming Judoon doesn't require me to have a higher level of knowledge. Mr. Truetemp's belief about the temperature is arguably sufficient for reliabilists to produce a lower level of knowledge, just as you're justified in knowing that you're hungry, or a dog is justified in knowing it's going for a walk when the leash appears.

Reliabilism isn't the only option. As McCain discusses, Evidentialism offers the intuitively plausible claim that you know when your belief fits the evidence to which you have access. When you have evidence for a belief, then you're justified in believing it; and when your evidence is insufficient, you're unjustified. Unlike reliabilism, which focuses on how external objects are perceived, Evidentialism focuses on the internal states of our minds. A reliabilist would say you know you see the TARDIS when your perception of the TARDIS is reliably formed, and you can further justify your belief (at a higher level) by examining the big blue box that you believe is the TARDIS. For an evidentialist, however, your perception of the TARDIS is evidence for your belief, because your internal mental states are of perceiving the TARDIS. Of course, there might counterevidence that would discount the truth of your belief: You might be sick and hallucinating, you might be on a movie set, you might have forgotten that *Doctor Who* is just a TV show—Is it? So, for Evidentialism, beliefs are justified when you have good evidence for a belief.

Another Internalist theory of justification is coherentism. Inspired by the criticism that the basic beliefs of foundationalism are arbitrary, coherence theory argues that beliefs are justified when they form a "web" of mutually supporting, internally coherent beliefs. As we'll see in the next section, some epistemologists complain that coherentism is fundamentally flawed—if each belief justifies the other, then each belief justifies itself; in other words, coherentism's justification is based on circular reasoning. McCain explains that such a criticism would only be true, if beliefs were understood in a linear fashion, where an individual belief A justifies B, B justifies C, and C justifies A. This is circular reasoning and should be avoided. However, coherentism avoids circularity by maintaining that beliefs are justified as a whole. Instead of focusing on the truth of individual beliefs, all beliefs should be examined as a coherent whole; and when all beliefs cohere (fit together in a reasonable way), then each individual belief is justified.

The Infinity of Knowledge

Before concluding the chapter, I want to make a case for a theory of justification that I think the Doctor would be inclined to accept, or at least zie would be fascinated by its cleverness. Over the past two decades, Peter Klein has argued for infinitism, which he maintains avoids the criticisms of foundationalism, knowledge resting on arbitrary beliefs, and coherence theory, the circularity of beliefs. We just saw how arbitrariness of belief can be ignored by employing reliabilism, so we can focus on circularity.

In one of Klein's more recent writings he implies the necessity of reliabilism for knowledge, but in terms of explaining the nature of human knowledge, which is a distinct feature of human knowledge, he maintains that human epistemic agents should be capable of calling on and giving reasons for why they hold certain beliefs over others. Because Klein limits the requirements of infinitism to the distinctive nature of human knowledge, which will apply to all other similar creatures, he doesn't diminish the knowledge of non-human creatures. As noted above, this is an important implication for any description of the *Doctor Who* universe. For Klein, then, in order to have a justified set of reasons, and to avoid the circularity of a belief justifying itself (I saw the TARDIS because I saw the TARDIS), our justifications must be based on an infinite number of non-repeating beliefs.

To avoid circularity, infinitism doesn't allow a person to reuse beliefs. If we can't reuse beliefs, then we must have access to an infinity of beliefs to justify our knowledge. This is a major problem, since we, as humans, are finite creatures. Due to the nature of infinity, we could spend our entire life reciting the set of all whole numbers, and we would never reach the "end," since the set of all numbers is infinite. Herein lies the cleverness of Klein's infinitism: the complaint that finite creatures can't accomplish an infinite task is based on a "completion requirement," which as Jeremy Fantl shows in "Modest Infinitism," justification not only comes in degrees, but infinitism doesn't have such a completion requirement.

Infinitism is more interested in the process than the end, which sounds a lot like our favorite Time Lord, who hates endings too. Infinitism takes into account human finiteness, and relies on the human imagination to examine beliefs for defeaters in order to arrive at knowledge. Infinitism's reliance on the imagination is one of the reasons I think the Doctor would be so intrigued by its methods.

The human brain is continually active, whether we're aware of it or not. We're constantly perceiving the world, while our brains actively process the data from our senses. Even if we're just wandering around on "autopilot," our brain is aware and constantly testing our perceptions. Just think of watching a *Doctor Who* episode, and how easy it is to relax and get lost in the story without being aware of your surroundings or the common "noises" in your head. Whether on a lower or higher level of reasoning, humans have at their disposal an infinite number of propositions that can test any belief. You could never access them all, but infinitism doesn't require that you be capable of doing so.

Let's see how this works. If you lived in Britain during the 1950s and 1960s, seeing a blue police box wouldn't be surprising. You would perceive them on a lower level without giving them a second thought, because your brain would be trained to perceive them as part of the natural surroundings. Fast forward to today, and seeing a police box, whether you're a fan of *Doctor Who* or not, instantly kicks your mind into high gear, asking: What is it? Is it a TARDIS? Is it real? Is it a fan creation? Is there a convention in town? Are they filming in town? Is this what I've been waiting for my whole life; the Doctor's come to ask me to become a companion?

All of these and more illustrate how we use the imagination to start asking questions about what's being perceived. The mind is looking for defeaters, some sort of explanation that will help you understand and know what you're seeing. Granted, many of the questions would be outlandish, like "Is it car? Is it a book? Is it the number 2," but nevertheless, they all serve to justify your belief in what you see? The mind doesn't have to actually ask every question, but thanks to the imagination, it has the capacity, if given an infinity of time, for an infinite amount of questions.

As Jacob Bronowski suggests in *The Origins of Knowledge and Imagination*, human language allows for individuals to become the subject of his or her own sentence. We are able to place ourselves in our own "box," and our imaginations give us the ability to reach out into an infinity of "open spaces." These open spaces are new ideas and beliefs generated by the imagination, which allow us access to an infinite number of positive and negative possibilities. It's this imaginative approach—placing oneself in a "box" to achieve infinity— that makes me think the Doctor would find infinitism most intriguing.

Why Is Knowledge Relevant?

So, what are the practical lessons that follow from thinking about reality and knowledge?

First, there's nothing wrong with being ignorant, but we should never be willfully ignorant. The more information we have, the better decisions we'll make about how to live our lives. So, the more knowledge, the better. If you lack knowledge, or you don't know what counts as knowledge, you'll struggle to know anything. Hopefully, what we have been discussing will aid in your search for truth and help you understand when you know something, or when you need to spend more time searching.

Second, the reliabilism of Alston's foundationalism and the imagination of Klein's infinitism suggest an engaged life of seeking and questioning. This implication is at the heart of the Doctor's other lessons, so it should be at the heart of our philosophical lesson.

Third, we can't always determine truth and knowledge by ourselves. We need the help of others. As communal beings we often arrive at an understanding of questions through what John Hardwig calls "knowledge-as-trust." Hardwig is most interested in how knowledge is generated in a scientific community through the reliable transference of data and information between multiple parties, but his conclusion applies to all human interaction. Knowledge requires that we listen, test, and ultimately trust that if we're careful enough we can come to have knowledge.

Finally, there's a certain virtue to seeking knowledge. As Linda Zagzebski shows, an accurate engaged search for truth and knowledge is more than just a task. Courageously seeking truth and knowledge and not shying away from difficult questions and answers is a sign of a virtuous character, while ignoring tough questions and blindly running away from truth and knowledge illustrates a poor character. The Doctor calls us to work towards the former in all that we do, regardless of whether it's in terms of ethics, art, or knowledge.[1]

---

[1] A special thank you to Jared Byer, who inspired and suggested the addition of this chapter, and Kevin McCain for his invaluable comments and insights.

Epilogue

Though not officially part of the Whoniverse, Rick pretty much sums up my feelings about *Doctor Who*. No matter the situation, struggle, or disaster, my goal is always to approach life as the Doctor. When I do, I know there's nothing that can stand in my way. There's no one and no thing that can keep me down. Nothing can prevent me from doing what needs doing. Even if I fail miserably, I know everything will be all right. No, it'll be better than all right. It'll be fantastic!

You see, *Doctor Who* is much more than a quirky television show about a time-traveling alien. I know too many people who credit *Doctor Who* with why they're alive today. They found something in the Doctor that gave them hope to live. No matter the mountain, the Doctor gave them strength and motivation to keep climbing, and as a result, the world is a better place. This is the "secret" message that's communicated to those who watch *Doctor Who*. You are IMPORTANT, you are VALUABLE, and the world is a sadder place without YOU. As humans, we tend to seek the path of least resistance, yet we're happiest when working hard to achieve a goal. The Doctor teaches us to be engaged, and it's through the struggle to engage that we find ways to be fantastic. We all make the world a better place when we dedicate ourselves to being fantastic. We become happier, we help others be happier, and as a result, the world is happier. Was this the original goal of Verity Lambert and the other early creators of *Doctor Who*? No, but they saw the show's potential, and decided they would do whatever it took to ensure the show's production and success. The torch they lit continues to shine as bright and strong today as it did in 1963, whether on television, in books, comics, and fan-created art, conventions, books, and magazines, and everything in between.

As I finish writing this book, Jodie Whittaker has finished her second season, and though the fandom seems overly fractured, I have no worries that *Doctor Who* will continue to broadcast its message of engagement, compassion, and critical thinking into the future. The word 'fan' is simply short for 'fanatic', and we shouldn't be surprised that fanatics don't always think straight. Add to the mix fans' ability to have their voice heard twenty-four-hours a day via social media, blogs, and every other Internet platform imaginable, and it's easy to feel as if the Whoniverse is crumbling in on itself.

There's no need to worry. There have been complainers and distractors throughout *Doctor Who*'s history. In fact, fan passion and conviction, whether hailing or complaining, is an illustration of how fans live the lessons of the Doctor. Except for those who lack the social skills required to have a discussion without reverting to name-calling and bullying, expressing one's joy and disappointment is part of living the engaged life. We love and hate because we care, and it's this love and hate that inspires fans and creators to do better and be better.

Though we might choose to ignore (or unfollow) some fans, we should still delight in their passion and celebrate their freedom to express themselves. We might not agree, or we might be totally opposed to their opinions, but remember, the Doctor teaches that we're all important. If the Doctor is correct, then even the most annoying fan is worthy of respect, and by extension, their opinion is valuable. As Voltaire once wrote, "I disapprove of what you say, but I will defend to the death your right to say it." Your freedom is important, because who you are is the direct result of what you do with your freedom. We can choose to do nothing, and our lives will lack valuable relationships and experiences. We can choose to be Daleks, hating everything that is not us. We can choose to be Cybermen, bent on making everyone like us by destroying difference. We can choose to the Master/Missy, using other people as pawns in our selfish schemes. Or, we can choose to be the Doctor (or at least one of zirs companions), engaging, helping, and striving to be fantastic. My goal with this book was to provide some fun and insightful explanations for how to more-easily achieve a life of the Doctor.

You Were Fantastic . . .

This journey is coming to an end, but you're just beginning a new one. If what I've said is true, then I began this book in 1983 during my first experience watching *Doctor Who* with my grandfather, and though I've had my ups and downs over the past (almost) forty years, it's been fantastic. Life, and the joys contained within every experience, are often taken for granted. The desire to travel back in time, and use what you know now to make better decisions, is the fundamental realization that life can go better or worse depending on the choices we make. The Doctor shows us that it's pointless trying to go back into our own time-stream in order to change the past. Look at what happens to Rose in "Father's Day" (2005). Trying to change the past is futile. Even in "The Day of the Doctor" (2013) the Doctor doesn't really change the past. If he'd erased the past, then he'd have no memory of the events between the Ninth Doctor and the Eleventh (2005-2013). At the end of "The Day of the Doctor" the Doctor would've been a completely different person, unrecognizable by viewers and to zirself.

Instead of erasing the past, the Doctor created a new timeline: one in which zie still has the memories of the children he killed, yet one in which he also prevented those deaths. (I know it's confusing. See Massimo Pigliucci's "Could the Doctor Have Avoided Trenzalore?" in *More Doctor Who and Philosophy* for an explanation for how it can happen.) The lesson we must keep in mind is that we can't change the past, but we can take advantage of every last millisecond of the life we have *now*.

Wisdom is NOT about memorizing facts, being rich, having influence, or winning arguments. Wisdom is about truth. And though we fill our lives with many "truths" (truths of mathematics, who won the Super

Bowl, what's the Doctor's real name), the "truth" of life can't be known, can't be found in formulas, and can't be achieved simply by doing what others tell us to do. The "truth" of life must be lived, and it requires a certain amount of trust in yourself and others around you. It should, then, be no surprise that both *truth* and *trust* come from the same root word *trēowe.*

No matter what fills your life with meaning, explains your existence, or motivates you to act, they all require trust—trust that you're acting correctly and trust that your actions will result in living a good life. The more we discover about the nature of reality through science, the more we should be in awe of what we don't know. The more we're inspired through religion, "the holy," and shows like *Doctor Who*, the more we should thirst for science and knowledge. Every question and discovery should generate new sets of questions, which paradoxically means, the more we learn and understand the less we know with certainty.

Do you really care about truth or do you just want to prove yourself right? Truth is the focus of *Doctor Who*, while the latter is the life of the fool. The easiest lie in the world is the one you tell yourself to justify your desire to be right. Do you want to live a meaningful life? If you do, then you'd better focus on truth, or you'll find yourself so lost, you'll learn nothing. Are you scared of being wrong? If you are, good. You should be scared, and excited by the possibilities of the unknown. As the Third Doctor says, courage is "being afraid and doing what you have to do anyway" ("Planet of the Daleks," 1973). We're all wrong from time to time, but it's only through being wrong and growing from our mistakes that we mature and understand truth.

I hope something in the previous pages will help you along your journey, and if we're both lucky, I hope our paths cross one day. Until then, may your TARDIS always take you where you need to go, and may you find peace in all you do. Farewell, fond companion . . .

Filmography

Doctor Who

"An Unearthly Child" (1963)
"The Edge of Destruction" (1963)
"The Daleks" (1963)
"Marco Polo" (1964)
"The Aztecs" (1964)
"Dalek Invasion of Earth" (1964)
"The Romans" (1965)
"The Tenth Planet" (1966)
"The Moonbase" (1967)
"Evil of the Daleks" (1967)
"Enemy of the World" (1968)
"The War Games" (1969)
"Spearhead from Space" (1970)
"The Silurians" (1970)
"The Claws of Axos" (1971)
"Planet of the Daleks" (1973)
"The Green Death" (1973)
"Time Warrior" (1973)
"The Planet of Spiders" (1974)
"Genesis of the Daleks" (1975)
"The Invisible Enemy" (1977)
"Robots of Death" (1977)

"The Invasion of Time" (1978)
"City of Death" (1979)
"Logopolis" (1981)
"Castrovalva" (1982)
"Snakedance" (1983)
"The Five Doctors" (1983)
"Frontios" (1984)
"Resurrection of the Daleks" (1984)
"The Caves of Androzani" (1984)
"Attack of the Cybermen" (1985)
"The Trial of a Time Lord" (1986)
"Dragonfire" (1987)
"Remembrance of the Daleks" (1988)
"The Happiness Patrol" (1988)
"Battlefield" (1989)
"Survival" (1989)
Doctor Who: TV Movie (1996)
"The End of the World" (2005)
"The Unquiet Dead" (2005)
"The Long Game" (2005)
"Father's Day" (2005)
"The Parting of the Ways" (2005)
"School Reunion" (2006)
"The Rise of the Cybermen" (2006)
"Age of Steel" (2006)
"The Impossible Planet" (2006)
"Love and Monsters" (2006)
"Runaway Bride" (2006)
"Shakespeare Code" (2007)
"Gridlock" (2007)
"Evolution of the Daleks" (2007)
"Blink" (2007)
"Last of the Time Lords" (2007)
"Fires of Pompeii" (2008)
"Planet of the Ood" (2008)
"The Poison Sky" (2008)
"The Sontaran Stratagem" (2008)
"Midnight" (2008)

"Journey's End" (2008)
"The End of Time" (2009–2010)
"The Beast Below" (2010)
"Victory of the Daleks" (2010)
"Flesh and Stone" (2010)
"The Vampires of Venice" (2010)
"Cold Blood" (2010)
"A Christmas Carol" (2010)
"The Doctor's Wife" (2011)
"The Almost People" (2011)
"The Rebel Flesh" (2011)
"Dinosaurs on a Spaceship" (2012)
"A Town Called Mercy" (2012)
"Hide" (2013)
"The Crimson Horror" (2013)
"Nightmare in Silver" (2013)
"The Night of the Doctor" (2013)
"The Day of the Doctor" (2013)
"The Time of the Doctor" (2013)
"Into the Dalek" (2014)
"Flatline" (2014)
"Dark Water" (2014)
"Death in Heaven" (2014)
"The Last Christmas" (2014)
"Kill the Moon" (2014)
"Deep Breath" (2014)
"Listen" (2014)
"The Witch's Familiar" (2015)
"Hell Bent" (2015)
"Heaven Sent" (2015)
"The Lie of the Land" (2017)
"The Woman Who Fell to Earth" (2018)
"Rosa" (2018)
"Kerblam!" (2018)
"The Witchfinders" (2018)
"It Takes You Away" (2018)
"Spyfall" (2020)
"The Timeless Children" (2020)

Star Trek

"Who Watches the Watchers" (1989)
"The Inner Light" (1992)
Star Trek: Insurrection

Bibliography

Alston, William. 1976. Two Types of Foundationalism. *Journal of Philosophy* 73.7.

Aristotle. 1962 [circa 335–323 B.C.E.]. *Nicomachean Ethics*. Translated by Martin Ostwald. New Jersey: Prentice Hall.

———. 2001. *The Basic Works of Aristotle*. Edited by Richard McKeon. Introduction by C.D.C Reeve. New York: The Modern Library; first published by Random House, 1941.

Asimov, Isaac. 1966 [1951]. *Foundation*. New York: AvonBooks.

Baxendale, Trevor. 2009. *Prisoner of the Daleks*. London: Random House UK.

Bentham, Jeremy. 1988 [1789]. *The Principles of Morals and Legislation*. Amherst: Prometheus Books.

Bertland, Alexander. 2010. Doctor Who as Philosopher and Myth Maker. In Lewis and Smithka 2010.

Bronowski, Jacob. 1978. *The Origins of Knowledge and Imagination*. New Haven: Yale University Press.

Burdge, Anthony, Jessica Burke, and Kristine Larsen. 2010. *The Mythological Dimensions of Doctor Who*. Crawfordville: Kitsune.

Cahn, Stephen. 2008. *Exploring Philosophy of Religion: An Introductory Anthology*. Oxford: Oxford University Press.

Crome, Andrew, and James F. McGrath. 2013. *Time and Relative Dimensions in Faith: Religion and Doctor Who*. London: Darton Longman, and Todd.

Decker, Kevin S. 2013. *Who Is Who? The Philosophy of Doctor Who*. London: Tauris.

Fantl, Jeremy. 2003. Modest Infinitism. *Canadian Journal of Philosophy* 33.4.

French, Peter A. 1997. *Cowboy Metaphysics: Ethics and Death in Westerns*. Lanham: Rowman and Littlefield.

———. 2001. *The Virtues of Vengeance*. Lawrence: University Press of Kansas.

Gandhi, Arun. (Accessed July 2015). "A Recollection." <www.google.com/url?sa=t&rct=j&q=&esrc=s&source=web&cd=1&ved=0CB8QFjAA&url=http%3A%2F%2Fwww.panoreon.gr%2Ffiles%2Fitems%2F3%2F365%2Fa_recollection_dr_arun_gandhi.pdf&ei=ZhygVfjrDsmS-wHJ-YCQBQ&usg=AFQjCNFnC27Ifqk1m92BnRjDxAbzVYdHCw&sig2=2wMCDnyeBvZksJhE-Cje_A&bvm=bv.96952980,d.cWw>.

Gettier, Edmund L. 1963. Is Justified True Belief Knowledge? *Analysis* 23.

Gladstone. (Accessed July 2015). "How *Doctor Who* Became My Religion." <www.cracked.com/blog/how-dr.-who-became-my-religion/>.

Glover, Jonathan. 2012. *Humanity: A Moral History of the Twentieth Century*. Second edition. New Haven: Yale University Press.

Green, Bonnie, and Chris Willmott. 2013. The Cybermen as Human.2. In Hills 2013.

Griffiths, Paul. 2003. Religion. In Taliaferro and Griffiths 2003.

Hansen, Christopher J., ed. 2010. *Ruminations, Peregrinations, and Regenerations: A Critical Approach to* Doctor Who. Newcastle upon Tyne: Cambridge Scholars.

Hardwig, John. 1991. The Role of Trust in Knowledge. *Journal of Philosophy* 88:12.

Hardwig, John, Nat Hentoff, Daniel Callahan, Felicia Cohn, Joanne Lynn, and Larry R. Churchill. 2000. *Is There a Duty to Die? And Other Essays in Bioethics*. New York: Routledge.

Held, V. 2006. *The Ethics of Care: Personal, Political, and Global*. Oxford: Oxford University Press.

Hick, John. 2010 [1966]. *Evil and the God of Love*. New York: Palgrave Macmillan.

Hills, Matt, ed. 2013. *New Dimensions of Doctor Who: Adventures in Space, Time, and Television*. London: Tauris.

Holley, David M. 2010. Meaning and Mystery: What It Means to Believe in God. Malden: Wiley-Blackwell.

Hopfe, Lewis M. and Mark R. Woodward. 2011. *Religions of the World*. Twelfth edition. New York: Pearson.

Hume, David. 2000 [1739]. *A Treatise of Human Nature*. Edited by David Fate Norton and Mary J. Norton. Oxford: Clarendon.

Jaggar, Alison M., and Iris Marion Young, eds. 2000. *A Companion to Feminist Philosophy*. Malden: Blackwell Publishing.

James, William. 1984. *William James: The Essential Writings*. Edited by Bruce W. Wilshire. Albany: State University of New York Press.

Kant, Immanuel. 1981 [1785]. *Grounding of the Metaphysics of Morals*. Translated by J. Ellington. Indianapolis: Hackett.

Kierkegaard, Søren. 1973. *A Kierkegaard Anthology*. Edited by Robert Bretall. Princeton: Princeton University Press.

Kiss, E. 2000. Justice. In Jaggar and Young 2000.

Klein, Peter D. 1998. Foundationalism and the Infinite Regress of Reasons. *Philosophy and Phenomenological Research* 58:4.

———. 1999. Human Knowledge and the Infinite Regress of Reasons. *Philosophical Perspectives* 13, Supplement of *Epistemology* 33.

———. 2003. When Infinite Regresses Are *Not* Vicious. *Philosophy and Phenomenological Research* 66:3.

———. 2007. Human Knowledge and the Infinite Progress of Reasoning. *Philosophical Studies* 134.

Kuhn, Thomas S. 1996 [1962]). *The Structure of Scientific Revolutions*. Third edition. Chicago: University of Chicago Press.

Kurtz, Paul. (1983). *In Defense of Secular Humanism*. New York: Prometheus.

Lehrer, Keith. 2000. Externalism and Epistemology Naturalized. In Sosa, Kim, and McGrath 2000.

Lewis, Courtland. 2010. Philosophy, *Fantastic!* In Lewis and Smithka 2010.

———. 2010. Cybermen Evil? I Don't Think So. In Lewis and Smithka 2010.

———. 2013. Why Time Lords Do Not Live Forever: Immortality in *Doctor Who*. In Crome and McGrath 2010.

———. 2013. Understanding Peace within Contemporary Moral Theory. *Philosophia: Philosophical Quarterly of Israel*. 41:4.

Lewis, Courtland, and Paula Smithka, eds. 2010. *Doctor Who and Philosophy: Bigger on the Inside*. Chicago: Open Court.

———, eds. 2015. *More Doctor Who and Philosophy: Regeneration Time*. Chicago: Open Court.

Mann, George. 2013. *Engines of War*. New York: Broadway.

McCain, Kevin. (2016). *The Nature of Scientific Knowledge: An Explanatory Approach*. Switzerland: Springer International Publishing.

Melville, Herman. 1992 [1851]. *Moby-Dick: Or, The Whale*. New York: Modern Library.

Middleton, Harry. 1989. *The Earth Is Enough: Growing Up in a World of Flyfishing, Trout, and Old Men*. Boulder: Pruett.

Mill, John Stuart. 2002 [1861]. *Utilitarianism*. Edited by George Sher. Cambridge: Hackett.

Milgram, Stanley. 1983. *Obedience to Authority*. New York: Harper Perennial.

Nietzsche, Friedrich. 1968. *The Will to Power*. Edited by Walter Kaufmann. Translated by Walter Kaufmann and R.J. Hollingdale. New York: Hackett.

———. 2000. *Basic Writings of Nietzsche*. Translated by Walter Kaufmann. New York: Modern Library.

Nozick, Robert. 2013 [1974]. *Anarchy, State, and Utopia*. New York: Basic Books.

Otto, Rudolf. 1923. *The Idea of the Holy*. Translated by John Harvey. Oxford: Oxford University Press.

———. 2003. The Numinous. In Taliaferro and Griffiths 2003.

PBS Idea Channel. (Accessed July 2015). Is *Doctor Who* a Religion? <www.youtube.com/watch?v=3Csjr8bXvPw>.

Pigliucci, Massimo. 2015. Could The Doctor Have Avoided Trenzalore? In Lewis and Smithka 2015.

Plato. 1990. *The Theaetetus of Plato*. Indianapolis: Hackett.

———. 1999 [1961]. *The Collected Dialogues of Plato, Including the Letters*. Seventeenth edition. Edited by Edith Hamilton and Huntington Cairns. Princeton: Princeton University Press.

———. 2004. *Plato's Meno*. Newburyport: Focus/Pullins.

Rawls, John. 1955. Two Concepts of Rules. *Philosophical Review* 64.

Reeves-Stevens, Judith, and Garfield Reeves-Stevens. 1990. *Star Trek: Prime Directive*. New York: Pocket Books.

Robb, Brian. 2009. *Timeless Adventures: How Doctor Who Conquered TV*. London: Kamera.

Siler, R. Alan. 2015. Magnetic North. In Lewis and Smithka 2015.

Silvia, J.J. 2010. Doctor, Who Cares? In Lewis and Smithka 2010.

Singer, Peter. 2001. *Writings on an Ethical Life*. New York: Harper Perennial.

Sleight, Graham. 2012. *The Doctor's Monsters: Meanings of the Monstrous in Doctor Who*. New York: Tauris.

Smart, Ninian. 2008. The Dimension of Religion. In Cahn 2008.

Sosa, Ernest, Jaegwon Kim, and Matthew McGrath, eds. 2000. *Epistemology: An Anthology*. Malden: Blackwell.

Taliaferro, Charles, and Paul Griffiths, eds. 2003. *Philosophy of Religion: An Anthology*. Malden: Blackwell.

Taylor, Charles. 2007. *A Secular Age*. Cambridge: Harvard University Press.

Thomas, Laurence Mordekhai. 1993. *Vessels of Evil: American Slavery and the Holocaust*. Philadelphia: Temple University Press.

Tillich, Paul. 1957. *Dynamics of Faith*. New York: Harper and Row.

Tipton, Scott, and David Tipton. 2013. *Prisoners of Time*. San Diego: IDW.

Wilken, Robert Louis. 2003. *The Christians as the Romans Saw Them*. New Haven: Yale University Press.

Wolterstorff, Nicholas. 2008. *Justice: Rights and Wrongs*. Princeton: Princeton University Press.

———. 2011. *Justice in Love*. Emory University Studies in Law and Religion. Grand Rapids: Eerdmans.

Nicholas Wolterstorff, Mark R. Gornik, and Gregory Thompson, eds. 2011. *Hearing the Call: Liturgy, Justice, Church, and World*. Grand Rapids: Eerdmans.

Zagzebski, Linda T. 1996. *Virtues of the Mind: An Inquiry into the Nature of Virtue and the Ethical Foundations of Knowledge*. Cambridge Studies in Philosophy. Cambridge: Cambridge University Press.

Zimbardo, Philip. (Accessed 2015). Stanford Prison Experiment. <www.prisonexp.org/>.

Index

DAVE CHAPPELLE
AND PHILOSOPHY
WHEN KEEPING IT WRONG
GETS REAL

Edited by Mark Ralkowski

This book has not been prepared, authorized,
or endorsed by *Dave Chappelle.*

Dave Chappelle and Philosophy
When Keeping It Wrong Gets Real

VOLUME 1 IN THE OPEN UNIVERSE SERIES,
POP CULTURE AND PHILOSOPHY®

Edited by Mark Ralkowski

"Dave Chappelle. Truth-teller or out of touch? Progressive or retrograde? Timeless or tired? Feminist or misogynist? Ally or apologist? Iconic or infamous? The philosophers gathered here confront these questions and more, offering readers a deeper appreciation of Chappelle's art and a better understanding of Chappelle as an artist."

—SHEILA LINTOTT, Professor of Philosophy, Bucknell University

"Hunkered down in our various ideological bunkers, we live certain in our knowledge of who's on our side and who's the enemy. Dave Chappelle is unique in his ability to make us laugh while scrambling the lines, making everyone uncomfortable. This is also what good philosophy does. Put the two together and the result is this volume."

—STEVEN GIMBEL, author of *Isn't That Clever: A Philosophical Account of Humor and Comedy* (2020)

"This wonderful collection approaches Chappelle as 'the most talented comedian in the world' and humor as 'one of the most valuable things in life'. Explaining why we're drawn to Chappelle's comedy despite its flaws, this remarkable study of the value of comedy, its relationship with truth, and its ties with freedom succeeds in unraveling the unique job of comedy through a close and engaging analysis of a controversial phenomenon in contemporary culture."

—LYDIA AMIR, Tufts University, author of *The Legacy of Nietzsche's Philosophy of Laughter* (2021)

MARK RALKOWSKI is the editor of *Louis C.K. and Philosophy: You Don't Get to Be Bored* (2016) and *Curb Your Enthusiasm and Philosophy: Awaken the Social Assassin Within* (2012). He is the author of *Plato's Trial of Athens* (2018) and *Heidegger's Platonism* (2009).

ISBN 978-1-63770-002-0 (paperback)

ISBN 978-1-63779-003-7 (ebook)

AVAILABLE FROM ALL BOOKSTORES AND ONLINE BOOKSELLERS

For more information on Open Universe books, go to
www.carusbooks.com